M000045816

Insights You Need from
Harvard
Business
Review

CRYPTO

Insights You Need from Harvard Business Review

Business is changing. Will you adapt or be left behind?

Get up to speed and deepen your understanding of the topics that are shaping your company's future with the **Insights You Need from Harvard Business Review** series. Featuring HBR's smartest thinking on fast-moving issues—blockchain, cybersecurity, AI, and more—each book provides the foundation introduction and practical case studies your organization needs to compete today and collects the best research, interviews, and analysis to get it ready for tomorrow.

You can't afford to ignore how these issues will transform the landscape of business and society. The Insights You Need series will help you grasp these critical ideas—and prepare you and your company for the future.

Books in the series include:

Agile

Artificial Intelligence

Blockchain

Climate Change

Customer Data and Privacy

Cybersecurity

The Future of Work

Global Recession

Hybrid Workplace

Monopolies and Tech Giants

Racial Justice

Strategic Analytics

The Year in Tech, 2021

The Year in Tech, 2022

The Year in Tech, 2023

Web3

CRYPTO

Harvard Business Review Press
Boston, Massachusetts

Printed in the United States of America

10 9 8 7 6 5 4 3 2 1

Library of Congress Cataloging-in-Publication Data

Names: Harvard Business Review Press, issuing body.
Title: Crypto.
Other titles: Crypto (Harvard Business Review Press) | Insights you need from Harvard Business Review.
Description: Boston, Massachusetts : Harvard Business Review Press, [2023] | Series: Insights you need from Harvard Business Review | Includes index.
Identifiers: LCCN 2022034369 (print) | LCCN 2022034370 (ebook) | ISBN 9781647824495 (paperback) | ISBN 9781647824501 (epub)
Subjects: LCSH: Cryptocurrencies. | NFTs (Tokens) | Smart contracts. | Blockchains (Databases)
Classification: LCC HG1710.3 .C77 2023 (print) | LCC HG1710.3 (ebook) | DDC 332.4--dc23/eng/20220923
LC record available at https://lccn.loc.gov/2022034369
LC ebook record available at https://lccn.loc.gov/2022034370

ISBN: 978-1-64782-449-5
eISBN: 978-1-64782-450-1

The paper used in this publication meets the requirements of the American National Standard for Permanence of Paper for Publications and Documents in Libraries and Archives Z39.48-1992.

Contents

Section 3
The Road to Web3

Introduction

LOOKING BEYOND CRYPTO BOOMS AND BUSTS

by Jeff John Roberts

I first encountered cryptocurrency in the summer of 2013 when, as a young tech reporter, I covered a Bitcoin meetup in leafy Union Square Park in New York City. I didn't expect much—maybe some tables set up with people buying and selling muffins and T-shirts—but what I found instead was something very different. In a corner of the park, a motley crew of scruffy anarchists and well-dressed bankers flashed QR codes and $100 bills. They were trading Bitcoin in the open air, and despite their wildly different backgrounds, they were united in celebration of this new digital money. The vibe felt less like the outdoor flea market I had expected and more like a cross between a religious gathering and an underground currency market. Some of these true believers were wary of my presence, but most were keen for the opportunity to draw another person into a movement they were convinced would change finance and the world. They had dubbed their corner of the park "Satoshi Square" after the anonymous founder of Bitcoin, which was going for $70 apiece at the time.

That December, Bitcoin soared to a previously unimaginable $1,100 only to suffer a brutal crash a few months later along with a handful of other cryptocurrencies such as the long-forgotten Peercoin and Feathercoin. The crash delighted the early crypto skeptics, who took it as proof that digital currency had been a hype-driven scam all along. But even at this time, a few steadfast crypto-entrepreneurs were quietly laying the groundwork for the next boom cycle they were sure would come.

This sequence of events has since repeated twice with bigger numbers each time—most recently in 2021 when Bitcoin shot to a high of $67,000, only to tumble by more than two-thirds in the spring of 2022 along with the rest of the crypto market. This boom-and-bust cycle, with troughs known as a "crypto winter," has become familiar, but over the course of each cycle, the world of crypto has changed dramatically.

For starters, after the crash in 2013, the cryptocurrency market was valued at around $8 billion. Even in the doldrums of early 2022, the overall market stood at $1 trillion—more than all but a handful of the biggest *Fortune* 500 companies. Meanwhile, the technology underlying crypto has evolved at a dizzying speed. The ascendance of Ethereum in 2016 triggered an explosion of smart contract activity, and more recently, the industry has created giant new markets in fields like decentralized finance (DeFi) and non-fungible tokens (NFTs).

Another big change from 2013 is how the media and the rest of the world view crypto. A decade ago, the debate pitted a small cohort of zealous believers against a larger chorus of skeptics and detractors, but the vast majority of people didn't know or care about crypto in the first place. Today, a healthy portion of the population owns crypto in the form of a token or an NFT, and nearly everyone—especially in the business world—has a basic understanding that blockchain technology is important, even if they aren't sure exactly how it works.

As crypto has entered the mainstream, the debate surrounding it has become more sophisticated and nuanced—and now transcends the binary view that crypto must be either the world's salvation or simply a scam. A case in point is the collection of smart articles in this book, which span a wide variety of topics, but all shed light on why crypto matters (and sometimes doesn't) in the context of business.

The volume is grouped into three sections that, in turn, examine the meaning of crypto tokens, real opportunities for NFTs, and the emerging world of Web3—a term that describes a potentially massive shift in the architecture and power structure of the internet. In "How DAOs Could Change the Way We Work," tech author Steve Glaveski explores this evolution, explaining how decentralized autonomous organizations offer radical new forms of governance and corporate incentives. He quotes venture capitalist and crypto theorist Chris Dixon saying that if Web 1.0 was "read only" and Web 2.0 is "read-write," then the third iteration of the internet—Web3—will be "read-write-*own*." For the first time, consumers will own and control important parts of the internet thanks to blockchain.

This idea of new types of web-based ownership is central to the opening pieces of the book, which reveal how trading in digital tokens amounts to much more than a speculative casino. Columbia professor Omid Malekan provides an especially helpful guide on this subject. In "To Understand Crypto's Volatility, Think About It as a Startup," he shows how tokens offer a new type of early-stage equity—functioning in the same way as private shares, but also providing groundbreaking forms of liquidity and price discovery. In this sense, blockchain technology has the potential to be vastly superior to legacy financial systems that are often slow, clumsy, and opaque.

Crypto: The Insights You Need from Harvard Business Review also offers plenty of practical advice for executives who might encounter crypto propositions at work and need to know if these amount to real opportunities or mere hype. Some of these insights come in the form of a traditional case study in which the CFO of an online education company must decide whether to endorse the crypto-obsessed CEO's call to add crypto to the balance sheet. The case study includes responses from real-life executives, including Amrita Ahuja, the CFO of payments giant Block (formerly Square, which renamed itself in a nod to blockchain in 2021).

Readers already steeped in blockchain will be pleased to see some big names from the crypto world among the authors. Nic Carter, an influential venture capitalist, describes the environmental impact of Bitcoin—a pressing topic for executives in a corporate world concerned with ESG issues—in a thoughtful and dispassionate fashion.

Carter's analysis points out, correctly, that energy use and carbon emissions are not synonymous and that judging a blockchain's environmental impact involves weighing competing moral priorities.

And while some of the authors in this collection are blockchain evangelists, the volume also offers some refreshing notes of caution. This includes software engineer Molly White's skeptical take that many blockchain projects are "a solution in search of a problem," and Stern School of Business professor Arun Sundararajan's advice that companies not embarrass themselves by diving too heavily into crypto lingo in their communications (co-opting NFT slang in social media posts will backfire, he reminds us, "so go easy on those WAGMIs").

Overall, this book will help you keep up to speed on a crypto industry that is constantly changing and transforming itself. This includes providing an overview of the biggest ideas from the most recent crypto boom and also tactical suggestions for day-to-day business decisions. The articles are also sprinkled with important Web3 words and products—such as Axie Infinity, P2E, and Snapshot—that readers should at least be conversant with, even if they don't try them firsthand.

Most significantly, *Crypto: The Insights You Need from Harvard Business Review* will help readers understand how crypto fits into the business world and society at large. A growing number of people are becoming convinced that this is an important technology, like the advent of the World Wide Web in the mid-1990s, but struggle to explain exactly why or how to make money from it. This era saw startups like WebVan and Pets.com spend millions on Super Bowl ads only to go bankrupt months later. In hindsight, it's clear that they had the right ideas—that's why we have the likes of DoorDash and Chewy today—but did something wrong when it came to timing and execution. Some of the names listed in this book may go down as the Pets.com of our time, while others may grow to become as ubiquitous as Amazon or eBay—two early web companies that survived the crash and *did* figure it out. It's too early in crypto's development to predict with certainty which enterprises, applications, and business models will harness blockchain to remake the internet, but this book provides us with the context and analytic tools to make a better guess.

In describing crypto and Web3, I like to invoke the story of the blind scientists who have never seen an elephant but must try to identify it only by touch. One, holding the trunk, believes the creature must be like a snake. Another, touching a leg, thinks it must be some sort of tree. And so on, with the scientists arguing into the night. When it comes to predicting what the next phase of crypto will look like, we are in a similar predicament. While we can see parts—cryptocurrencies, NFTs, DAOs—we find it hard to see the whole. But after reading this book, the mystery that is crypto comes a little more into focus.

Section 1

CRYPTOCURRENCY FOR REAL

1

WHO WRITES THE RULES OF DECENTRALIZED FINANCE?

by Jake Ryan

Dogecoin, the joke currency that minted millionaires overnight. CryptoKitties, the digital trading cards of cartoon cats that have sold for over $100,000. A Pringles "flavor" that only exists as a non-fungible token (NFT) and sells for, well, a lot more than chips you can actually eat. On the face of it, these blockchain-based projects can sound absurd—baffling to the general public and mocking to the financial establishment. They're spoofs and pranks that sometimes make money. But if you can look past the inside jokes, jargon, and goofy names, you'll see that there's serious work happening in crypto. A community of developers and investors is building a solid, sustainable infrastructure that will undergird an entirely new kind of economy: a decentralized economy. Part of the decentralized economy is building an open, decentralized financial system (DeFi).

DeFi is young and evolving in productive (if sometimes confusing) ways. There is too much live experimentation going on to reliably predict what might come next. However, a growing market suggests that the fundamental innovations of blockchain—and the cryptography and software innovations that made it possible—are here to stay.

While much of the focus on cryptocurrencies has been on price speculation, the bigger game is still unfolding. The decentralization and automation that cryptocurrencies enable are transformational because they allow for new ways to create and transfer value. When artificial intelligence (AI), the internet of things (IoT), robotics, and cryptocurrency converge, the cluster of innovations create the possibility for something new—autonomous operations, or business processes that run themselves. The rules of this new system are being written right now, often by users who hold "governance tokens," which let them determine the direction in which these systems will evolve. For forward-looking companies and individuals who are working with crypto, these often-overlooked tokens have a particular value: a say in what comes next.

The Value of a Vote

There are two important concepts to crypto ecosystem architecture: decentralization and on-chain governance. Let's start with decentralization. Blockchain is an autonomous, peer-to-peer ledger technology for managing and recording transactions. Built for accuracy, transparency, and autonomy, blockchains eliminate the need for third-parties or fee-taking intermediaries—the verification is built into the software. Users do not have to deal with gatekeepers or fees and don't need to request permission to use this public infrastructure. Permissionless access to public blockchains fundamentally transforms the architecture of how we design financial transactions and financial system infrastructure. Because blockchains are immutable, that is, you cannot edit or alter a record, it means trust of a third-party is no longer required. And this innovation alone reduces fee and friction. (See the sidebar "How Blockchain Works.")

How Blockchain Works

by Marco Iansiti and Karim R. Lakhani

Here are five basic principles underlying the technology:

1. *Distributed database.* Each party on a blockchain has access to the entire database and its complete history. No single party controls the data or the information. Every party can verify the records of its transaction partners directly, without an intermediary.
2. *Peer-to-peer transmission.* Communication occurs directly between peers instead of through a central node. Each node stores and forwards information to all other nodes.
3. *Transparency with pseudonymity.* Every transaction and its associated value are visible to anyone with access to the system. Each node, or user, on a blockchain has a unique 30-plus-character alphanumeric address that identifies it. Users can choose to remain

anonymous or provide proof of their identity to others. Transactions occur between blockchain addresses.

4. *Irreversibility of records.* Once a transaction is entered in the database and the accounts are updated, the records cannot be altered, because they're linked to every transaction record that came before them (hence the term "chain"). Various computational algorithms and approaches are deployed to ensure that the recording on the database is permanent, chronologically ordered, and available to all others on the network.
5. *Computational logic.* The digital nature of the ledger means that blockchain transactions can be tied to computational logic and in essence programmed. So users can set up algorithms and rules that automatically trigger transactions between nodes.

Adapted from "The Truth About Blockchain" in *Harvard Business Review*, January–February 2017 (product #R1701J).

Then there's on-chain governance, which mediates how the rules that govern activity on a particular blockchain are set and revised. This could be used for constructing a decentralized autonomous organization (DAO) or a DeFi system. Our current financial system depends on trusted intermediaries, like mortgage brokers or bank presidents—they establish protocols and rules that protect the institution itself and the consumer. In a decentralized, blockchain-based financial system, this process of writing rules is often done through the use of on-chain governance. Early adopters using a new DeFi service can buy (or earn) governance tokens, which give the holder the right to vote on how the blockchain is maintained, upgraded, and managed. One token, one vote.

These tokens tend to come into play *after* a crypto-network is established. Most blockchain projects start with what's called "off-chain governance," which can mean anything from developers trading emails about how to change the code to founders passing notes in GitHub. The people who build the currency write a founding set of rules. Many go on to establish on-chain governance and utilize governance tokens.

Once that switch is flipped, governance tokens can become extremely valuable. It happened for Compound Finance, an early notable DeFi project where users earned governance tokens and the value of that token rose dramatically when the system went live on their mainnet. On-chain governance is more formal and democratic than off-chain, and it allows every governance-token holder the right to vote on decisions and choices that will guide the particular blockchain ecosystem. Some ecosystems may vote on features to be released. It could be the setting of monetary policy or the reserve requirements of collateral on a loan. Or it could be what type of consensus mechanism the blockchain uses, which affects performance, resource usage, and security for that blockchain. The on-chain governance structure is designed to maintain transparency because everyone can see the proposals and see the computation of results of a vote—and avoid back-room deal making.

While the primary focus of crypto investors has so far been speculation on appreciation, governance tokens will likely become more important—and valuable—as crypto investing matures. As the value of a crypto-network increases, so too does the value of the right to govern it. Because token holders must hold the crypto asset to continue to vote in the interests of that particular ecosystem, investors are going to want to obtain and hold more tokens so that they can continue to participate in the governing. As long as the ecosystem makes good decisions and offers a good and competitive service, the token will likely accrue more value as time goes on.

There is something analogous in the traditional financial system. If traditional equity provides a right or claim to cash flows after all business expenses are paid, then governance tokens are somewhat analogous to equity in that they confer a right to control the direction of a crypto-network and its treasury.

A Token with Rights

If you have a cellphone, you are a potential crypto investor or user. But it's not as simple as opening up a Coinbase account: A smart investor will ignore the gimmicky products that make news and take the time to educate themselves on the fundamentals of crypto. Because they come with a right to help shape the future of cryptocurrencies, governance tokens will likely become more important as crypto investing becomes more sophisticated.

We're entering a world where more and more is being done with less and less. Part of the reason that's possible is technology as innovation is at the heart of the economy. The world is becoming more automated. And as that trend continues, we're going to need mechanisms that manage the boundary between people and machine. In DeFi, the systems of on-chain governance and the use of governance tokens look quite promising. Crypto is still in its adolescence. The meme coins should be taken for what they are—a joke. But let's not confuse nonsense with the true innovation. The only crypto asset that gives its holder an explicit right is a governance token. Let us participate, not just speculate. Governance tokens give investors not just a stake, but a say. As we've seen throughout history, the right to vote is a powerful thing.

Despite intense focus on the rapidly fluctuating market price of cryptocurrencies, another asset—governance tokens—offers investors value beyond the possibility of buying low and selling high.

- ✓ Early adopters of new decentralized finance (DeFi) services may be able to buy or earn governance tokens on these platforms.
- ✓ Governance tokens give owners the right to vote on how the blockchain is maintained, upgraded, and managed. One token equals one vote.

- ✓ As cryptocurrency becomes more sophisticated and more integrated into the economy, those who hold governance tokens will have the ability to shape the future of DeFi.

Adapted from "Who Writes the Rules of a Blockchain?" on hbr.org, July 23, 2021 (product #H06HGR).

2

TO UNDERSTAND CRYPTO'S VOLATILITY, THINK ABOUT IT AS A STARTUP

by Omid Malekan

Spring of 2022 was a dark time for the crypto industry. Between April and June, Bitcoin's value more than halved; other coins fell even more. The Terra-UST ecosystem, which paired a crypto coin with one designed to be pegged to the dollar, collapsed, wiping out $60 billion worth of value and leading to cascading failures among crypto lenders. Established companies like Coinbase, a popular crypto exchange, announced layoffs.

Amid the turmoil, crypto skeptics doubled down on their critiques, often with a focus on the speculative excess, and argued that the crash revealed crypto as a Ponzi scheme. As evidence, some cited the extreme volatility. How could crypto live up to the hype if participation feels like a rollercoaster—one whose operator is opposed to safety inspections? While some of the criticism is well deserved, the focus on price volatility isn't as strong an argument as critics might think. Rather, it reveals a misunderstanding of what different crypto assets represent.

Crypto is a young industry. Most projects are barely five years old. Eventually, different coins are meant to serve different functions, but they all more or less act as startup equity with the distinctive properties of having liquidity and price discovery from the start. This unique attribute—enabled by the novelty of the underlying infrastructure—leads to a more benign explanation of the volatility.

Equity, Liquidity, and Volatility

Startup equity is a core concept in business. Everything from a venture capital investment in a software company to an ownership stake in your cousin's new restaurant falls into that category. But traditional startup equity has no liquidity—you don't invest in a restaurant with the hope of flipping your shares a month later. No liquidity means no price discovery, either. Your investment is hard to value.

Crypto is different because a token can start trading right away—sometimes even before the function the token is meant to be used for is live. This feature is enabled by crypto's underlying infrastructure, designed for a post-digital world where data roams freely and important tasks are performed by code, not clerks. This doesn't mean every project has to issue a token right away, but many do.

Early liquidity has benefits and drawbacks. Before analyzing them, it might help to understand why the legacy financial system doesn't offer this option, even to those who may prefer it.

Despite becoming more digital, the architecture of the Wall Street–run system is the same as it was decades ago. It relies on opaque systems that don't talk to each other and still require a good deal of manual processing. Trading may look hyperactive, but back-office settlement is a bottleneck, leading to access being restricted to the shares of the biggest companies. Regulations also play a role in this gatekeeping, but infrastructure is the primary bottleneck. The startup boom of the past decade has led to the creation of bespoke markets for smaller companies, but they too are limited in scope. Most companies can't issue liquid shares, even if they wanted to.

The natively digital design of a blockchain platform like Ethereum empowers it to handle more assets by orders of magnitude—hundreds of thousands (and soon to be millions) of tokens that can trade around the clock. Code automates how tokens are issued, traded, and transferred from one owner to the next. All assets are programmable, improving how different assets interact, reducing errors. Fractional ownership is easily accommodated, and universal access to the infrastructure is granted to entrepreneurs and investors alike. If this were the media industry, then Ethereum would be to Wall Street what YouTube was to cable TV, for better and for worse. Better infrastructure and a lack of gatekeepers result in greater participation and innovation, but the lack of curation means more garbage, too.

These features enable cheaper-to-operate and more-dynamic markets, and in some cases financial models that would not exist otherwise. The added efficiency comes with tradeoffs, however. On the one hand, capital formation improves, and entrepreneurs can tap a larger pool of potential investors. But an unavoidable consequence of bringing such enhanced efficiency to the shares of any young project is extreme volatility.

Most startups fail and investing in one is making a bet. From the entrepreneur's point of view, every decision—what kind of food should a new restaurant serve—has an amplified impact. So do outside developments, like getting a liquor license. From the investor's point of view, trying to discount the consequences of these decisions is equally daunting. The distribution of eventual outcomes for any business is widest at birth, so rational investors have no choice but to constantly overreact.

If your cousin's new restaurant had tradable shares, they'd probably be as volatile as crypto. Landing a liquor license might make them quadruple, while a bad review may make them tank. Given the uncertainty, external developments would also have an amplified impact. A new restaurant is more vulnerable to things like dining fads or bad weather than an established one.

Everything Is Bigger on Blockchain

Crypto investors grapple with a stronger version of this phenomenon because everything is borderless, and the total addressable market is huge. Unlike a new community bank, a blockchain-based lending protocol could theoretically serve hundreds of millions of people all over the world. Success could mean significant value accrual to its token, but the project could also fail. Early investors have no choice but to flail back and forth between hope and despair.

Their dilemma is compounded by the fact that most digital assets can't be pigeonholed into traditional categories, making valuation that much harder. Traditional investors can always rely on established metrics like a stock's price to earnings (PE) ratio for a sanity check. Crypto investors have no such option. Most digital assets are a hybrid and transition from one category to another throughout their life cycle.

Ether, for instance, started as a security, as its coins were sold up front to fund development. But once the blockchain launched, it transitioned to being a cross between a currency and a commodity. Some people used it as a store of value or medium of exchange, while others used it to pay for transaction validation and code execution. These features distinguished it from traditional equity and commodities—you can't pay for a cab ride with Uber stock, and you don't save in oil. Today, it has evolved even further to a yield-bearing instrument, a collateral asset for borrowing, a reference currency for NFTs, and the means by which validators participate in consensus.

All of these attributes make it difficult to assess the value of even the most mature crypto project, never mind the thousands that have launched recently. A skeptic could argue that these challenges are the very reason why nascent projects should not have tradable equity. Indeed, access to startup investing in traditional finance is often restricted to institutional and "sophisticated" investors. But such restrictions have their own drawbacks.

Lack of access to startup investing has contributed to the growing wealth gap. Successful companies like Meta (Facebook) stayed private for as long as possible, and VC funds still can't take retail money. Other investments like real estate or collectible art had too high an entry price for most people. Bitcoin was the lone exception, the only high-performing asset that was universally accessible and fractionally ownable from day one.

Bitcoin was still volatile during that period, but volatility isn't always bad. Price swings communicate important information to founders and investors, particularly during the crucial adolescent stage of any startup. And restricting price discovery to periodic funding rounds negotiated with a handful of investors can be dangerous. WeWork famously raised money at a $47 billion valuation less than a year before it ended up flirting with bankruptcy; Theranos was valued at $9 billion before going bust. Despite multiple red flags for both companies, there was little price information until the bitter end. Both investments turned out to be as volatile as crypto; we just couldn't see the volatility—and concerned investors couldn't get out.

The Good News About Bad News

Universal access, immediate price discovery, and greater transparency also contribute to both the reality and the perception of scams and shady behavior in crypto. Like any technology that removes friction, the ease with which new projects can be launched has been a boon to con artists and fly-by-night operators, in the same way that the accessibility and efficiency of email led to a spike in supposed princes looking for a place to park their money.

That's not to say that the failure rate of crypto projects isn't higher than new restaurants—new industries naturally have a lower success rate than established ones. But it is safe to assume that the rate in crypto is not as high as it seems. But total transparency makes crypto *look* worse than it is. Disingenuous entrepreneurs raising money from unsuspecting marks is an ancient practice in every industry. Thousands of new restaurants fail every year, and some of those failures inevitably turn out to be scams. But those investments aren't debated on Twitter, and we can't watch their shares collapse on a public website. Crypto is unique in that even the scams are transparent, and in the long run, transparency is a powerful tool for countering shady behavior, in any industry.

The crypto industry has a lot of growing up to do, and downturns offer hard lessons. Understanding what volatility means in crypto markets—what signals it's sending and responding to—is an integral step in this process. Investors and entrepreneurs are learning not only what is possible in this new ecosystem, but also what isn't, and why some of the lessons learned by the sectors that crypto hopes to disrupt transcend technology. Money and hubris make for a bad mix, and nothing reinforces the importance of humility better than a crash. But the skeptics who constantly harp on the volatility would be well advised to not fall into a similar trap, conflating necessary growing pains with a fatal condition.

One of the leading criticisms of crypto is its high volatility. But this argument misses important insights about how crypto assets differ from those in traditional finance.

- ✓ While different coins are designed to serve multiple functions, they all act as startup equity for future practical applications.

- ✓ Unlike traditional startup equity, which is usually held privately for years, crypto assets have liquidity and price discovery baked in from the start, making them more sensitive to signals and changes.
- ✓ The overlooked benefit of volatility is that price swings communicate important information to founders and investors and build previously unseen levels of transparency into the system.
- ✓ Crypto assets do fail at a high rate, they are volatile, and they are subject to downturns—and crypto investors are still learning what delivers value in this new ecosystem.

Adapted from "What Skeptics Get Wrong About Crypto's Volatility," on hbr.org, July 6, 2022 (product #H074Q0).

3

HOW DIGITAL CURRENCIES CAN HELP SMALL AND MEDIUM-SIZED BUSINESSES

by Shai Bernstein and Christian Catalini

Over the last few years, the development of blockchain technology brought us new types of digital assets such as stablecoins and cryptocurrencies. These innovations offer the foundations for building new payment rails that can move value across the globe not only in real time but also at a much lower cost. Unlike cryptocurrencies such as Bitcoin or Ethereum, stablecoins are significantly less volatile as they are typically pegged to a fiat currency such as the U.S. dollar. Stablecoins also pushed governments to accelerate their exploration of central bank digital currencies (CBDCs). While cryptocurrencies rely on decentralized networks for their operations, CBDCs would run on public-sector infrastructure and represent a direct liability of the central bank—essentially "digital cash."

There's major potential here: Digital assets and cryptocurrencies can support new services and create more competition in financial services. For one, they promise lower-cost payments for both domestic and cross-border transfers. They can also facilitate real-time payments, overcoming a significant shortcoming of the U.S. payment system. Moreover, these new assets support programmability, which can be used for conditional payments and more complex applications such as escrow.

At the same time, these technologies—and how they threaten traditional financial intermediaries—has ignited a heated debate that boiled over in early 2022. For example, a widely anticipated paper by the Federal Reserve Board acknowledged the significant benefits of digital currencies, but also raised concerns around privacy, operational, cybersecurity, and financial stability risks.[1] Similarly, Gary Gensler, chair of the U.S. Securities and Exchange Commission, nearly doubled his crypto enforcement staff to crack down on what he calls the "wrongdoing in the crypto markets."[2] Then the collapse of UST, Terra's stablecoin—one of the largest stablecoins—illustrates how a failure in one of these systems can cascade throughout the crypto ecosystem. While many stablecoins derive their value from being fully backed by reserves, that was not the case for UST, which instead relied on an algorithm and a second currency, Luna, for stability.

While these events underscore that the risks cryptocurrencies entail cannot be ignored, it is also clear that the status quo does not provide a satisfactory answer. The question is who carries the burden of an expensive, outdated, and slow payment system. This chapter surfaces the potential impact on small and medium-sized businesses, which embed significant consequences for economic growth and stability.

Small businesses—including restaurants, plumbers, and dry cleaners—play a critical role in our economy. They employ roughly half of all working Americans, amounting to more than 60 million jobs.[3] They created 65% of net new jobs from 2000 through 2019, represent 97.5% of all exporting firms in the United States, and account for 32% of known exported value.[4] Moreover, small businesses are also an essential vehicle for intergenerational mobility and social inclusion, offering upward mobility and economic opportunity, particularly for underrepresented groups.

Small businesses are also finding new ways to reach consumers outside their local communities through digital platforms such as Shopify and Amazon, a distribution channel that was vital for them during the pandemic to counter the decline in retail sales.

Nevertheless, they have largely been ignored during the debate over digital currencies. While policy makers, economists, and government officials highlight the importance of ensuring the resilience and growth of small businesses, the way they could benefit from a better and more competitive payments infrastructure is almost entirely overlooked.

The Financial Fragility of Small Businesses

Most small businesses operate with razor-thin cash buffers. The typical small business only holds enough cash to last less than a month. This leads to significant vulnerability to economic fluctuations, as illustrated by their collapse during the 2008 financial crisis and, more recently, the Covid-19 crisis. The latter carried devastating consequences for small businesses, forcing the government to issue an emergency Paycheck Protection Program (PPP) to ensure they could stay afloat.

There are many reasons for this, including their limited access to credit and the fewer financial options they have relative to larger firms. Small businesses are often considered riskier for lenders because they struggle to deliver the types of quantifiable metrics large banks expect when evaluating creditworthiness. While small businesses have relied more on community banks, bank consolidations have further limited this source of funding.

One of the most pressing issues for small businesses is payment delays. Large buyers, such as Walmart and Procter & Gamble, commonly use "buy now pay later" practices with their suppliers, with payment delays between 30 and 120 days. When applying such practices, large buyers are essentially borrowing from small businesses, significantly increasing their working capital needs and lowering their available cash buffers. Indeed, survey evidence suggests that almost 70% of small businesses that rely on invoices report cash flow problems linked to these payment delays.[5]

The challenges in accessing credit, combined with delayed payments, make it hard for small businesses to maintain healthy cash buffers, increase their exposure to economic shocks, and limit their ability to make investments. Increased competition and innovation in payments could improve their long-lasting resiliency and opportunity for growth.

How Slow and Expensive Payments Hurt Small Businesses

Most U.S. consumer payments are made via credit cards, a trend that accelerated during the Covid-19 pandemic. While entirely invisible to customers, merchants pay fees—to card-issuing banks, card-network assessment, and payment processors—that can reach above 3% of the transaction value. Online transactions, mainly through marketplace platforms such as Amazon or Shopify, can be even more expensive. Additionally, it can take several days to receive the funds, which increases working capital needs further.

All of this puts small businesses at a clear disadvantage. While large businesses can negotiate significantly lower fees when accepting digital payments, small businesses do not have much negotiating power. There are few alternatives to the major card networks, meaning that small businesses do not have a choice but to pass part of the fees to customers through higher prices, which lowers their ability to compete with deeper-pocket rivals.

These problems are magnified when dealing with cross-border transfers, where fees and delays are incredibly high. As of the second quarter of 2021, the average cost of sending a cross-border payment from the United States was 5.41%, fees were unpredictable, and SWIFT payments could take between one to five business days.[6] The complexity of the payment chain also makes international payments a target for scams and fraud.

How Blockchain Technology Can Help

To change this, we need a more open and competitive payments infrastructure. Critically important public-sector efforts such as FedNow and CBDCs need to be combined with private-sector innovation—including permissionless cryptocurrency networks. Public-sector efforts inevitably move at a glacial pace, and there is a real risk that they will be severely outpaced by innovation happening elsewhere, often within "walled gardens" that lock consumers and businesses into non-interoperable services.

But this does not have to be the case. The public sector can take advantage of the technical progress happening within the blockchain and cryptocurrency space to accelerate its journey toward real-time, low-cost payments.

An open payments system will drive competition, lower transaction fees, and unbundle the services that are currently part of all digital transactions—including those related to reversibility and chargebacks, intermediation, transaction risk assessment, and more—helping businesses pay only for what they actually need. Ideally, thanks to new forms of interoperability between digital wallets, banks, and legacy payment and card rails, small businesses would be able to do so without compromising which customers they can accept payments from. Moreover, transferring funds directly through a blockchain would benefit domestic and cross-border payments by reducing the number of intermediaries in the picture.

If this evolution of payments is successful, small businesses would experience not only lower costs but also faster access to funds. This would drastically improve their liquidity and cash buffers, and help them survive negative economic shocks and thrive.

By creating the right conditions for a truly open and interoperable protocol for money to emerge, very much like in the early days of the internet, the public sector can bring back competition to payments and give small businesses much-needed choice.

Small and medium-sized businesses work with tight margins, pay higher fees for payment processing, and suffer from cash flow problems as they wait to be paid for goods and services. Stablecoins and central bank digital currencies (CBDCs) could provide cheaper, more efficient payment systems.

- ✓ These technologies would allow small and medium-sized businesses to keep more of what they earn and significantly accelerate how quickly they get paid.
- ✓ Crypto could drastically improve small businesses' liquidity and cash buffers, helping them survive negative economic shocks and thrive.
- ✓ CBDCs will only be possible with public-sector support. Governments should take advantage of the technical progress happening within the blockchain and cryptocurrency space to accelerate its journey toward real-time, low-cost payments.

Adapted from "How Digital Currencies Can Help Small Businesses," on hbr.org, May 25, 2022 (product #H071DK).

NOTES

1. Board of Governors of the Federal Reserve System, "Money and Payments: The U.S. Dollar in the Age of Digital Transformation," January 2022, https://www.federalreserve.gov/publications/money-and-payments-discussion-paper.htm.

2. U.S. Securities and Exchange Commission, "SEC Nearly Doubles Size of Enforcement's Crypto Assets and Cyber Unit," press release, Washington, DC, May 3, 2022, https://www.sec.gov/news/press-release/2022-78.

3. Office of Advocacy, "2021 Small Business Economic Profile," U.S. Small Business Administration, n.d., https://cdn.advocacy.sba.gov/wp-content/uploads/2020/06/04144224/2020-Small-Business-Economic-Profile-US.pdf.

4. Office of Advocacy, "Frequently Asked Questions About Small Business, 2020," U.S. Small Business Administration, October 22, 2020, https://advocacy.sba.gov/2020/10/22/frequently-asked-questions-about-small-business-2020/.

5. "The Trade Credit Dilemma Report," PYMNTS and Fundbox, May 2019, https://www.pymnts.com/wp-content/uploads/2019/05/Trade-Credit-Dilemma-Report.pdf.

6. The World Bank, "Remittance Prices Worldwide Quarterly: An Analysis of Trends in Cost of Remittance Services," June 2021, https://remittanceprices.worldbank.org/sites/default/files/rpw_main_report_and_annex_q221.pdf.

HOW MUCH ENERGY DOES BITCOIN ACTUALLY USE?

by Nic Carter

Organizations around the world are facing pressure to limit the consumption of nonrenewable energy sources and the emission of carbon into the atmosphere. But figuring out how much consumption is too much is a complex question that's intertwined with debates around our priorities as a society. The calculation of which goods and services are "worth" spending these resources on, after all, is really a question of values. As cryptocurrencies, and Bitcoin in particular, have grown in prominence, energy use has become the latest flashpoint in the larger conversation about what, and who, digital currencies are really good for.

On the face of it, the question about energy use is a fair one. According to the Cambridge Center for Alternative Finance (CCAF), as of writing, Bitcoin consumes around 110 terawatt hours per year—0.55% of global electricity production, or roughly equivalent to the annual energy draw of small countries like Malaysia or Sweden.[1] This certainly sounds like a lot of energy. But how much energy *should* a monetary system consume?

How you answer that likely depends on how you feel about Bitcoin. If you believe that Bitcoin offers no utility beyond serving as a Ponzi scheme or a device for money laundering, then it would only be logical to conclude that consuming any amount of energy is wasteful. If you are one of the tens of millions of individuals worldwide using it as a tool to escape monetary repression, inflation, or capital controls, you most likely think that the energy is extremely well spent. Whether you feel Bitcoin has a valid claim on society's resources boils down to how much value you think Bitcoin creates for society.

If we're going to have this debate, however, we should be clear on how Bitcoin actually consumes energy. Understanding Bitcoin's energy consumption may not settle questions about its usefulness, but it can help to contextualize how much the environmental impact of Bitcoin really is. Specifically, there are a few key misconceptions worth addressing.

Energy Consumption Is Not Equivalent to Carbon Emissions

First, there's an important distinction between how much energy a system consumes and how much carbon it emits. While determining energy consumption is relatively straightforward, you cannot extrapolate the associated carbon emissions without knowing the precise *energy mix*—that is, the makeup of different energy sources used by the computers mining Bitcoin. For example, one unit of hydro energy will have much less environmental impact than the same unit of coal-powered energy.

Bitcoin's energy consumption is relatively easy to estimate: You can just look at its hashrate (that is, the total combined computational power used to mine Bitcoin and process transactions), and then make some educated guesses as to the energy requirements of the hardware that miners are using. But its carbon emissions are much harder to ascertain. Mining is an intensely competitive business, and miners tend not to be particularly forthcoming about the details of their operations. The best estimates of energy production geolocation (from which an energy mix can be inferred) come from the CCAF, which has worked with major mining pools to put together an anonymized data set of miner locations.

Based on this data, the CCAF can guess the energy sources that miners were using by country and, in some cases, by province. But their data set doesn't include all mining pools, nor is it up to date, leaving us still largely in the dark about Bitcoin's actual energy mix. Furthermore, many high-profile analyses generalize energy mix at the country level, leading to an inaccurate portrait of countries such as China, which has an extremely diverse energy landscape.

As a result, estimates for what percentage of Bitcoin mining uses renewable energy vary widely. In December 2019, one report suggested that 73% of Bitcoin's energy consumption was carbon neutral, largely due to the abundance of hydro power in major mining hubs such as Southwest China and Scandinavia.[2] On the other hand, the CCAF estimated in September 2020 that the figure is closer to 39%.[3] But even if the lower number is correct, that's still almost twice as much as the U.S. grid, suggesting that looking at energy consumption alone is hardly a reliable method for determining Bitcoin's carbon emissions.

Bitcoin Can Use Energy That Other Industries Can't

Another key factor that makes Bitcoin's energy consumption different from that of most other industries is that Bitcoin can be mined anywhere. Almost all of the energy used worldwide must be produced relatively close to its end users, but Bitcoin has no such limitation, enabling miners to utilize power sources that are inaccessible for most other applications.

Hydro is the most well-known example of this. In the wet season in Sichuan and Yunnan, enormous quantities of renewable hydro energy are wasted every year. In these areas, production capacity massively outpaces local demand, and battery technology is far from advanced enough to make it worthwhile to store and transport energy from these rural regions into the urban centers that need it. These regions most likely represent the single largest stranded energy resource on the planet, and it's no coincidence that these provinces are the heartlands of Bitcoin mining in China, responsible for almost 10% of global mining in the dry season and 50% in the wet season.

Another promising avenue for carbon-neutral mining is flared natural gas. The process of oil extraction releases significant amounts of natural gas as a by-product—energy that pollutes the environment without ever making it to the grid. Since it's constrained to the location of remote oil mines, most traditional applications have historically been unable to effectively leverage that energy. But Bitcoin miners from North Dakota to Siberia have seized the opportunity to monetize this otherwise wasted resource, and some companies are even exploring ways to further reduce emissions by combusting the gas in a more controlled manner. This is still a minor player in today's Bitcoin mining arena, but back-of-the-envelope calculations suggest that there's enough flared natural gas in the United States and Canada alone to run the entire Bitcoin network.

The monetization of excess natural gas with Bitcoin does still create emissions, and some have argued that the practice even acts as a subsidy to the fossil fuel industry. But given the reality that oil is and will continue to be extracted for the foreseeable future, exploiting a natural by-product of the process (and potentially even reducing its environmental impact) is a net positive.

The aluminum smelting industry offers a relevant parallel. The process of transforming natural bauxite ore into usable aluminum is highly energy intensive, and the costs of transporting aluminum often aren't prohibitive, so many nations with a surplus of energy have built smelters to take advantage of their excess resources. Regions with the capacity to produce more energy than could be consumed locally became net energy exporters through aluminum—and the same conditions have made those locations prime options for mining Bitcoin. There are even a number of former aluminum smelters, such as the hydro Alcoa plant in Massena, New York, that have been directly repurposed as Bitcoin mines.

Mining Bitcoin Consumes a Lot More Energy Than Using It

How energy is produced is one piece of the equation. But the other area where misconceptions are common is in how Bitcoin actually consumes energy, and how that's likely to change over time.

Many talk about Bitcoin's high "per-transaction energy cost," but this metric is misleading. The vast majority of Bitcoin's energy consumption happens during the mining process. Once coins have been issued, the energy required to validate transactions is minimal. Simply looking at Bitcoin's total energy draw to date and dividing that by the number of transactions doesn't make sense; most of that energy was used to mine Bitcoins, not to support transactions. And that leads us to the final critical misconception:

that the energy costs associated with mining Bitcoin will continue to grow exponentially.

Runaway Growth Is Unlikely

Because Bitcoin's energy footprint has grown so rapidly, people sometimes assume that it will eventually commandeer entire energy grids. This was the premise of a widely reported 2018 study, making the shocking claim that Bitcoin could warm the earth by two degrees Celsius.[4] But there's good reason to believe this won't happen.

First, as has become common in many industries, the energy mix of Bitcoin grows less reliant on carbon every year. In the United States, publicly traded, increasingly environmental, social, and governance–focused miners have been gaining market share, and China recently banned coal-based mining in Inner Mongolia, one of the largest remaining coal-heavy regions. At the same time, many organizations within the mining industry have launched initiatives like the Crypto Climate Accord—inspired by the Paris Climate Accords—to advocate for and commit to reducing Bitcoin's carbon footprint.

In addition, miners are unlikely to continue expanding their mining operations at the current rates indefinitely. The Bitcoin protocol subsidizes mining, but those subsidies have built-in checks on their growth. Today, miners receive small fees for the transactions that they verify while mining (accounting for around 10% of miner revenue), as well as whatever profit margins they can get when they sell the Bitcoins they have mined.

However, the protocol is built to halve the issuance-driven component of miner revenue every four years, so unless the price of Bitcoin doubles every four years in perpetuity (which economics suggests is essentially impossible for any currency), that share of miner revenue will eventually decay to zero. As for transaction fees, Bitcoin's natural constraints on the number of transactions it can process (fewer than a million per day) combined with users' finite tolerance for paying fees limit the growth potential of this as a revenue source.[5] We can expect some miners to continue operating regardless, in exchange for these transaction fees alone—and the network depends on that to keep functioning—but if profit margins fall, the financial incentive to invest in mining will naturally decrease.

. . .

There are countless factors that can influence Bitcoin's environmental impact, but underlying them is a question that's much harder to answer with numbers: *Is Bitcoin worth it?* It's important to understand that many environmental concerns are exaggerated or based on flawed assumptions or misunderstandings of how the Bitcoin protocol works.

That means that when we ask, "Is Bitcoin worth its environmental impact?" the actual negative impact we're talking about is likely a lot less alarming than you might think. But there's no denying that Bitcoin (like almost everything else that adds value in our society) does consume resources. As with every other energy-consuming industry, it's up to the crypto community to acknowledge and address these environmental concerns, work in good faith to reduce Bitcoin's carbon footprint, and ultimately demonstrate that the societal value Bitcoin provides is worth the resources needed to sustain it.

Bitcoin consumes as much energy as a small country. This may be alarming, but the reality is more complicated. To have the critical debate about whether the value of Bitcoin justifies its environmental impact, a more subtle look is required.

- ✓ Bitcoin *mining* requires more energy than Bitcoin *transacting*, and Bitcoin's protocol makes it likely that mining will peak and recede in the coming years, even as transactions grow.
- ✓ Energy consumption is not equivalent to carbon emissions. The carbon footprint of energy sources varies widely, and many Bitcoin mines are located near low-emission energy sources.
- ✓ Since Bitcoin can be mined anywhere, it can use excess energy that other industries can't, which otherwise would have gone unused.
- ✓ Ultimately, the crypto community must acknowledge and address environmental concerns, work in good faith to reduce Bitcoin's carbon footprint, and demonstrate the societal value that Bitcoin provides.

Adapted from "How Much Energy Does Bitcoin Actually Consume?" on hbr.org, May 5, 2021 (product #H06C5X).

NOTES

1. University of Cambridge, Cambridge Center for Alternative Finance, Cambridge Bitcoin Electricity Consumption Index (CBECI), July 2022, https://ccaf.io/cbeci/index.

2. CoinShares Research, *The Bitcoin Mining Network*, December 2019 Update, https://coinshares.com/research/bitcoin-mining-network-december-2019.es

3. Apolline Blandin et al., "3rd Global Cryptoasset Benchmarking Study," Cambridge University, Judge Business School, September 2020, https://www.jbs.cam.ac.uk/faculty-research/centres/alternative-finance/publications/3rd-global-cryptoasset-benchmarking-study/.

4. Camilo Mora et al., "Bitcoin Emissions Alone Could Push Global Warming Above 2°C," *Nature Climate Change* 8 (2018): 931–933.

5. Usman W. Choh, "The Limits to Blockchain? Scaling vs. Decentralization," Discussion Paper Series: Notes on the 21st Century, February 20, 2019.

5

CASE STUDY: SHOULD WE EMBRACE CRYPTO?

by Charles C. Y. Wang

The phone buzzed on the nightstand—once, twice, three times—waking Ankit Jain from what had been a restful sleep. Before he could reach the phone, three more texts came through. He knew who it would be: his boss, Thorsten Konig, the CEO of Ivory Tower, the world's leading online education platform.

In Sun Valley talking crypto.
It's time.

Payments + investment.
How fast can we do it?
Pls call ASAP to discuss.
Bring in Shira and Paul.

Ankit sighed. Thorsten was a brilliant technologist who had started and sold DayTradz, one of the first online retail trading platforms, before he was even 30. Ivory Tower was his second, also hugely successful, venture—one that was disrupting higher education by offering high-quality college and graduate-school courses to students around the world. Some, such as the intro to economics class taught by a Nobel Prize winner donating his time, were extremely affordable, while others, such as classes on personal branding with Kris Jenner and on M&A with Carl Icahn, were obscenely expensive. The idea was to have the platform's wealthiest users subsidize its poorest. The impact Ivory Tower had achieved in the five years since its launch—and in the 13 months since its IPO—was amazing. But sometimes being the CFO of a fast-moving company led by a "crazy genius" was exhausting.

For months now Thorsten had been talking about integrating cryptocurrency into the business. He was a huge proponent of Bitcoin and had put about 5% of his own portfolio into it. Several weeks ago, the CEO had asked Ankit to have his team look into accepting tuition payments and keeping some of Ivory Tower's cash reserves in crypto. In media interviews, Thorsten had also started alluding to "our crypto future," sparking speculation that he would build or buy a crypto trading platform. But Ankit knew that Thorsten was committed to Ivory Tower for at least the next few years; he just wanted to combine it with his new passion.

To Thorsten, taking fees and making investments in Bitcoin were simple matters—akin to doing business in euros as well as dollars, which Ivory Tower already did. Bitcoin adoption could allow the U.S.-based company to further hedge itself against dollar inflation.

Ankit knew that things were much more complicated. Although cryptocurrencies were gaining mainstream appeal, even established ones like Bitcoin were highly volatile, with value swings that made them look more like speculative stocks. Sure, it was possible to take payment in Bitcoin and then convert it to dollars, but the company had to figure out whether it made sense to build the internal capability needed or to hire a third-party vendor to handle transactions. And investing earnings in crypto was another thing entirely. Ankit's head hurt just thinking about the financial-reporting challenges. Then there was his fiduciary responsibility as CFO: Did shareholders really want Ivory Tower to bet on crypto if doing so might risk the capital needed down the road for developing better technology and courses and expanding the company's reach?

Unfortunately, Thorsten rarely took no for an answer. So Ankit rolled out of bed and texted his teammates. "Morning. T asking about crypto again. Zoom at 8 to discuss? He'll join at 8:30."

Within a minute, he'd received two thumbs up. By now everyone was used to Thorsten's impromptu meetings. Ankit just hoped this one wouldn't end with an edict.

Evaluating the Options

"I mean we *can* accept tuition payments in Bitcoin." Paul Abebe, Ivory Tower's controller, had jumped in immediately on the Zoom call. Everyone had been working from home since the start of the pandemic, and the company had decided it wouldn't require anyone to return to its Manhattan headquarters. "It's annoying—not as liquid as nondigital currencies, obviously. There would be IRS reporting and anti-money-laundering compliance issues to consider. But the question is: Why *should* we do it?"

"Thorsten says it fits with our ethos: embracing the future, spearheading new technologies, shaking up the stodgy educational community," Shira Peretz, Ankit's deputy, said. "Edo loves the idea too." She was referring to Edo Sanger, Ivory Tower's CMO. "He thinks it will make for great press."

"And will that translate into more users and revenues?" Paul asked skeptically. "What percentage of our students even care about this?"

"Well, our blockchain and crypto courses are actually some of our most popular, but Thorsten admits that at this point most people probably won't pay in Bitcoin," Ankit said. "He's more interested in investing our excess cash in it. Thoughts?"

"It's a terrible idea," Paul said.

"Agree," Shira said. "There's no GAAP guidance on how to account for this stuff yet. But the AICPA says Bitcoin isn't considered cash or a cash equivalent, inventory, or a financial instrument, so it needs to be treated like an intangible asset, which means that if its value falls, we have to mark it down on our balance sheet. But if it goes up, we report those gains only when we sell. So if we're meaningfully invested, we could be taking big, random hits to our net income for no business-related reason. Communicating the company's performance will get more complicated."

"But if Bitcoin goes up in the long run, could it give us gains that smooth out or boost profitability?" Ankit asked. "Our shareholders aren't looking for perfect quarterly results. They want us to invest wisely to grow the company."

"I'm sorry, but an asset that goes from a valuation of $60K to $30K in one month cannot be considered a prudent investment," Paul countered. "How do we know that Bitcoin will be worth as much next year as it is now? And will we use just Bitcoin or also Ether or any of the thousands of other cryptocurrencies?"

"For now, Thorsten's talking only about Bitcoin," Ankit said. "It has the largest user base and longest history. And he's convinced it will go up in value."

"If our shareholders want to bet on crypto, they can do it directly," Paul said. "When we filed our S-1 for the IPO, we didn't say anything about a Bitcoin treasury."

"Well, we'd disclose it, and investors could sell if they're not on board," Shira said. Then she shook her head. "But I agree that it's too soon, too volatile. I vote for accepting Bitcoin payments—if it's doable without too much compliance and IT complications. Investments, no."

"I'm a no and a no," Paul said.

Just then, Ankit saw that Thorsten was in the Zoom waiting room. "OK, guys, here comes T," he said, letting the CEO in.

"Hello, friends!" Thorsten said as his face popped up on-screen. "What a fabulous day to be talking about the future. Catch me up on our crypto plans."

Ankit took the lead. "We've evaluated our options, and while we appreciate the potential benefits of Bitcoin, we're going to advise against—"

"Aha! I knew you guys would say this. Your job is to worry about the spreadsheets. I understand. But that's why I'm here: to help you see the big picture. Bitcoin is the future. There is no world in which it underperforms relative to major currencies over the next decade. We have so much cash in reserves. Why wouldn't we put some of it into assets that produce high returns we could invest in the company? We could get appreciation up to 10 times what we'd otherwise see. We'll help propel Bitcoin forward and democratize the movement of money, just as we're democratizing education. We must do this!"

Ankit could tell that Paul and Shira were deflated, if not surprised. This did seem like a fait accompli. What Thorsten wanted, Thorsten usually got.

The Board's Concerns

After setting his team to work figuring out how to take crypto payments and spending a few hours modeling various levels of investment in Bitcoin, Ankit checked his email. Cindy Yu, the company's newest director and the head of its audit committee, had sent a message asking him to call her.

"Cindy, hi! I just saw your message. What's up?"

"Hi, Ankit. Thanks for getting back to me. I'm calling with some board concerns. Can we speak off the record?"

"Of course."

"Thorsten has mentioned to several directors that he's interested in making Bitcoin a bigger part of Ivory Tower's business. At the same time, he's personally—and not insignificantly—invested in Bitcoin. Some of us are worried that this at least has the appearance of a conflict of interest."

"I see."

"More important, some of us have questions about the wisdom of taking our treasury into crypto. Obviously, I expect that we'll discuss this at the board meeting next week, but I wanted to give you a heads-up. I suspect that Thorsten has asked you to present a plan to us. However, we want your candid opinion. He has his allies, of course. But as nonexecutive directors, we have to make decisions in the company's best interest, and we expect the finance team to make recommendations based on the same criteria."

"Of course."

"I know Thorsten is a force of nature and doesn't make it easy to disagree with him. But if you do, the board needs to hear it, and you will have our support."

Pressure from the CEO

At 7, Ankit was out for a jog when his phone rang: Thorsten.

"Ankit. Hope I didn't catch you at a bad time. I wanted to reconnect on crypto."

"Just on a run. No problem."

"Ah, keep running. I can talk as you go," Thorsten said. "I want you to know that I understand your hesitancy. And we can take it slow. But I have a track record of knowing what's next in business. First DayTradz, now Ivory Tower—both big successes, though many didn't believe they could be. You can trust me again now. Bitcoin has outperformed the dollar since its inception, is gaining popularity with our user base, and in my opinion will be more efficient and secure than regular currencies. Other cutting-edge companies are already starting to jump in. Now is the time for us to as well. Our support will help the crypto movement. We'll take power from large institutions and put it into the hands of the people. This fits perfectly with our mission."

Ankit wasn't sure how to reply, but Thorsten didn't press any further. "OK, continue your exercise, my friend. And tomorrow we'll run toward the future together!"

After the call, Ankit picked up his pace and tried unsuccessfully to zone out to his iPhone music. Was Thorsten right? If monetary exchange was going to move toward crypto, Ivory Tower should certainly get ahead of the shift. But what if governments clamped down on cryptocurrency? If Bitcoin lost all its value? The board members were right to ask hard questions. And Ankit wasn't at all sure how to answer them.

The Experts Respond: Should Ankit Back Thorsten's Bitcoin Plans or Not?

Amrita Ahuja is the CFO of Square

Ankit should support the push into Bitcoin—as both an accepted form of payment and an investment on the balance sheet. At Square we believe there's a high probability that the internet will have its own native cryptocurrency, and Bitcoin is the strongest contender. It's the most secure and resilient, with a principled, decentralized, transparent, and consensus-based development model. We foresee a future in which companies won't have to navigate fiat currencies and local rules and regulations that create complexity and high costs for consumer transactions across borders. Cost, time, and security inefficiencies will fall away, and companies that accept Bitcoin payments will be able to serve anyone in the world, including people who have historically been marginalized by financial systems or who distrust federal banks (as in Latin America and certain other regions). This fits perfectly with Ivory Tower's mission of bringing quality higher education to underserved communities globally, and the company should get ahead of the game.

Thorsten's also right that having Bitcoin on the balance sheet will demonstrate to customers, employees (present and future), shareholders, and onlookers that it has "skin in the game" and will help make a more inclusive internet currency a reality. In addition, Bitcoin can provide attractive diversification and act as an inflation hedge.

Square invested 5% of its cash and cash equivalents in Bitcoin. We believe that the long-term opportunity is worth any near-term volatility and that our investment will enable us to learn and help improve the system while increasing trust in it. To that end, Square has set up the Crypto Open Patent Alliance to increase access to cryptotechnology through a collaborative patent library; Square Crypto, an independent team solely focused on contributing to the Bitcoin open-source work; a $10 million Bitcoin clean-energy initiative to incentivize miners to use renewable sources; and a $5 million endowment to fund education about Bitcoin and promote its adoption.

Ivory Tower could similarly be at the leading edge of network development, building good relationships with regulators to enable consumer protection and address bad actors while also fostering innovation and figuring out how to master custody, insurance, exchange, accounting, payroll, tax reporting, and compliance.

Ankit, of course, needs to address all the concerns that his team and Cindy Yu have raised. But with Thorsten's support and a clear strategy and execution plan, he can make the case that the company has the opportunity to be at the forefront of this rapidly emerging trend. This is the time for him to truly lead as CFO.

Roxi Wen is the CFO of Invitae

The case *against* Ivory Tower's moving to accept and hold Bitcoin is far stronger than the one *for* it. Ankit should oppose the plan—but only after having a frank conversation with Thorsten to outline the downsides and explore other ideas.

Paul is right that cryptocurrency is too volatile to be of balance-sheet quality. If Ivory Tower wants an inflation hedge, many alternatives—gold and real estate, for example—are less risky. Moreover, managing Bitcoin transactions and custody will require the finance department to build entirely new capabilities, such as safe storage for Bitcoin keys, and it's unclear that that would be a good use of staff time. And the regulatory environment is extremely uncertain; difficult disclosure rules or divestment requirements could crop up at any time.

I also find it hard to believe people will want to pay tuition in Bitcoin. Most buyers of crypto want to hold it for capital appreciation and as an inflation hedge, just like Thorsten. Why would customers use their holdings to pay for courses, logging taxable capital gains now?

Thorsten thinks Bitcoin will be more secure and efficient than currencies backed by governments. But that's debatable, since fiat payments, particularly in developed countries, move securely and often more rapidly than Bitcoin blocks do.

Sure, Bitcoin may someday trade as frequently and easily as dollars, euros, and yen. Ivory Tower might get useful marketing value from being ahead of the curve and solidifying its reputation as a forward-looking innovator. However, given the complexities surrounding Bitcoin, I think there are more-effective ways to gain competitive advantage.

Ankit needs to artfully manage Thorsten. When you work with a smart, fast-moving leader who is full of ideas, you often feel your job is to constantly say no. But that's not a productive relationship. Instead, you want to have candid strategic conversations.

The two men should talk about what Thorsten really wants. Is it to embrace Bitcoin? Or to become part of the blockchain revolution? And if it's the latter, is there another way to deploy the technology in the business? For example, could it be used to set up an open, distributed operating system where users could create their own classes? Could payment collection happen via blockchain even when customers pay in traditional currencies? These are much broader questions, and Thorsten's answers might help Ankit find a way to honor the CEO's wishes without doing exactly as he says.

At my company my colleagues have lots of ideas about what to do with our significant cash reserves, but no matter how wild their suggestions are, I never just reject them. I sit down with people, ask what they're trying to accomplish, and brainstorm how to achieve those goals even if it's in ways different from what they've suggested. Ankit should do the same with Thorsten.

Of course, the CEO could put his foot down and persuade the board to back him. Elon Musk was able to do that with Bitcoin investments at Tesla. But even then, Ankit could pitch a lower-risk experiment—perhaps creating a small, separate holding company to test Bitcoin in.

The CFO has authority and credibility with Thorsten and the board. He shouldn't be afraid to use it.

Adapted from an article in Harvard Business Review, *November–December 2021 (product #R2106M). HBR's fictionalized case studies present problems faced by leaders in real companies and offer solutions from experts. This one is based on Charles C. Y. Wang and Siyu Zhang, "Accounting for Bitcoin at Tesla," Case 9-121-074 (Boston: Harvard Business School, 2021).*

Section 2

NFTs FOR BUSINESS

6

HOW NFTs CREATE VALUE

by Steve Kaczynski and Scott Duke Kominers

In March 2021, a work of art called *Everydays: The First 5000 Days* sold for $69 million at Christie's auction house. It's not out of the ordinary to see eight-figure art sales, but this one received a lot of attention because the piece was sold as a non-fungible token (NFT)—an electronic record corresponding to an image that lives entirely in the digital world.

Put differently: Someone paid almost $70 million for a picture on the internet.

Since then, NFTs have started to permeate pop culture in various ways. They've been spoofed by *Saturday*

Night Live and embraced by high-profile celebrities like rapper Snoop Dogg and NBA superstar Stephen Curry. As of this writing, there are hundreds of millions of dollars of NFT sales each week through public marketplaces like Foundation, OpenSea, and Nifty Gateway, as well as custom-built applications like NBA Top Shot and VeVe.

Yet at the same time many people wonder how tokens on the internet could be worth money at all—especially when many of them just represent "ownership" of an online image or animation that you could, in principle, download a copy of for free.

It's easy to see why NFTs inspire both excitement and deep skepticism: They're a completely novel asset class, and we don't see new asset classes appear that often. But what drives the value of an asset that's really just a digital token people can pass around? To appreciate NFTs properly, we first have to think through what they actually are and the types of market opportunities they enable. And once we unlock that, we can understand how to build businesses around them.

Disclosure: Both Kaczynski and Kominers own NFTs, as well as other crypto assets. Additionally, Kominers provides market design advice to a number of marketplace businesses and crypto projects, including Novi Financial, Inc., the Diem Association, koodos, and Quora.

NFTs as a Tool for Market Design

NFTs have fundamentally changed the market for digital assets. Historically there was no way to separate the "owner" of a digital artwork from someone who just saved a copy to their desktop. Markets can't operate without clear property rights: Before someone can buy a good, it has to be clear who has the right to sell it, and once someone does buy, you need to be able to transfer ownership from the seller to the buyer. NFTs solve this problem by giving parties something they can agree represents ownership. In doing so, they make it possible to build markets around new types of transactions—buying and selling products that could never be sold before or enabling transactions to happen in innovative ways that are more efficient and valuable.

Each NFT is a unique, one-of-a-kind digital item. They're stored on blockchains, which means it's possible to prove who owns a given NFT at any moment in time and trace the history of prior ownership. Moreover, it's easy to transfer NFTs from one person to another—just as a bank might move money across accounts—and it's very hard to counterfeit them. Because NFT ownership is easy to certify and transfer, we can use them to create markets in a variety of different goods.

But NFTs don't just provide a kind of digital "deed." Because blockchains are programmable, it's possible to endow NFTs with features that enable them to expand their purpose over time, or even to provide direct utility to their holders. In other words, NFTs can do things—or let their owners do things—in both digital spaces and the physical world.

In this sense, NFTs can function like membership cards or tickets, providing access to events, exclusive merchandise, and special discounts—as well as serving as digital keys to online spaces where holders can engage with each other. Moreover, because the blockchain is public, it's even possible to send additional products directly to anyone who owns a given token. All of this gives NFT holders value over and above simple ownership—and provides creators with a vector to build a highly engaged community around their brands.

It's not uncommon to see creators organize in-person meetups for their NFT holders. In other cases, having a specific NFT in your online wallet might be necessary in order to gain access to an online game, chat room, or merchandise store. And creator teams sometimes grant additional tokens to their NFT holders in ways that expand the product ecosystem: Owners of a particular goat NFT, for example, were able to claim a free baby goat NFT that gives benefits beyond the original token; holders of a particular bear NFT, meanwhile, just received honey.

Thus, owning an NFT effectively makes you an investor, a member of a club, a brand shareholder, and a participant in a loyalty program all at once. At the same time, NFTs' programmability supports new business and profit models; for example, NFTs have enabled a new type of royalty contract, whereby each time a work is resold, a share of the transaction goes back to the original creator.

This all means that NFT-based markets can emerge and gain traction quickly, especially relative to other crypto products. This is both because the NFTs themselves have stand-alone value—you might buy an art NFT simply because you like it—and because NFTs just need to establish value among a community of potential owners (which can be relatively small), whereas cryptocurrencies need wide acceptance in order to become useful as a store of value and/or medium of exchange.

The Advent of NFT Ecosystems

As marketplaces have sprung up around NFTs, creators have taken advantage of their possibilities in different ways.

The best-known examples are the digital art market, described above, and digital collectibles platforms, such as Dapper Labs's NBA Top Shot, which enables users to collect and exchange NFTs of exciting plays from basketball games—videos called "moments," which are effectively digital trading cards. Top Shot has been building in gamified challenges and other reasons to own the cards beyond just their pure collectible value, even teasing that moment holders may eventually receive real-world benefits from the NBA.

But what's emerged more recently is a model of active ecosystem-building around NFT-native properties—leading to novel organizations developed entirely within the NFT space. These products start with an NFT series but project forward a road map under which holders of the NFT gain access to an expanding array of products, activities, and experiences. Revenue from initial and subsequent NFT sales is fed back into the brand, supporting increasingly ambitious projects, which in turn drive up the value of the NFTs themselves.

The Bored Ape Yacht Club, for example, comprises a series of NFT ape images conferring membership in an online community. The project started with a series of private chat rooms and a graffiti board, and has grown to include high-end merchandise, social events, and even an actual yacht party. SupDucks and the Gutter Cat Gang similarly began building communities around NFT image series and associated online spaces; the former has bridged into a boardwalk-themed metaverse game, and the latter has focused on real-world benefits like extravagant in-person events.

People often take on membership in these collectives as part of their personal identity, even using their favorite NFT image as their public profile picture on social media. Each NFT community has different personalities and purposes, and there are so many by now that almost everyone can find a group they can call their own. In this way, NFT ownership provides an immediate shared text that people can use to connect with each other.

Moreover, in many of these communities, ownership also conveys partial or full commercial rights—or even some degree of governance in how the community is run—which means members can build properties on top of their NFTs that grow the value of the overall brand. Crucially, this creates a channel by which engaged fandom can feed back into the brand itself: "Jenkins the Valet" is a Bored Ape member-created project that has effectively become its own sub-brand. Individual SupDucks members have created art and character identities around their NFTs that have been absorbed into the SupDucks metaverse. And community-created fan projects have built out parts of the Gutter Cat Gang story arc.

All of these benefits make owning the associated NFTs more valuable—and almost paradoxically, this increase in the value of ownership comes in a form that helps separate the value of ownership from the purely financial opportunity of reselling.

Building on this phenomenon, a few well-known brands have recently introduced NFT series that serve to identify, reinforce, and expand their existing communities of brand enthusiasts. The popular streetwear brand The Hundreds, for example, has built an NFT project around its mascot the "Adam Bomb," and directly rewards its community of NFT holders with improved access to the brand through connection with the founders and early access to new product releases.

Many emerging NFT applications, meanwhile, are seeking to more explicitly blend online NFT ownership with offline use cases. A few restaurants, for example, have started using NFTs for reservations. And the ticketing industry has a major opportunity here: By issuing tickets as NFTs, venues can give a variety of benefits to purchasers, creating more of an incentive to buy, as well as providing the venues an opportunity to collect royalties on secondary sales.

Other companies are exploring how NFTs could be used in establishing and recording people's identity and reputation online. MIT recently started offering blockchain-based digital diplomas, which are effectively non-transferable NFTs. Meanwhile, both established players like Facebook (now Meta) and new ventures like POAP and koodos are providing ways for individuals to create and share NFTs around activities, affinities, and interests.

How These Businesses Can Succeed

Like all other businesses, each NFT project has to respond to a real market need. But there are unique challenges to building in the NFT space:

These ventures must make meaningful use of the NFT technology itself

It's not an accident that so many of the early NFT projects are built around digital rights management, since that's one of the most direct applications of the technology. Club membership benefits for NFT holders fit in naturally as well, since a given NFT holder can certify their right to have access simply by pointing to the token in their crypto wallet.

But NFTs make less sense when there isn't a purpose to digital ownership, such as for managing physical collectibles, where people presumably want to receive the objects themselves. (Unless, of course, they're too heavy to move, as in the case of an NFT for a 2,000-pound tungsten cube.)

NFTs also have to leverage a community of users

As with any new product, early adopters serve as product evangelists and a source of early feedback. But with NFTs, these users also serve an even more essential role: Their decision to embrace the NFTs quite literally imbues those NFTs with their meaning and establishes their initial value.

Without a robust community of users, NFT projects can fail to get off the ground, or can quickly collapse as all the token holders lose interest. And this means that if an NFT project doesn't make its value proposition clear enough at the outset, it can fail to recruit a big enough community—or the right community. Lack of engagement can then become a self-fulfilling prophecy, devaluing the NFTs themselves.

To maintain ongoing community engagement, NFT project teams must generate confidence that they can continue executing

In the world of crypto, where many people engage partially or completely anonymously, crises of confidence in a project can cascade quickly, which means it's particularly important that the team communicate frequently and transparently about how they intend to evolve the project. (Many NFT teams have frequent "community calls" for this purpose.)

Here NFT projects can also lean on established brands or institutions, as well as explicit promises of real-world utility. For example, a sports team or popular music artist selling tickets through NFTs can use their existing reputation and events infrastructure to convince people that the NFT tickets really do have value. That said, an existing company releasing an NFT without any specific purpose or value can look gimmicky and thus fail to create engagement.

NFT projects need accessible "on-ramps" for new users

NFTs also face a number of challenges that are general across crypto entrepreneurship. Most crypto technology at the moment is not user friendly, requiring interfacing with a number of abstruse cryptocurrency exchanges and wallet providers.

NBA Top Shot has benefited tremendously from submerging most of the underlying crypto structure in its NFT market and enabling users to purchase moments in fiat with credit cards, rather than requiring people to transact in cryptocurrency. Other projects have recruited onboarding directors to help first-time NFT consumers navigate the process of purchasing.

An NFT project needs to be able to weather crypto market swings

Additionally, crypto markets are volatile, and the surrounding regulatory frameworks are still being sorted out. These market swings can dramatically change the demand for NFTs, which again underscores the importance of building community and other sources of direct value for NFT ownership.

Outlook

As with any novel asset class, the future of NFTs is uncertain. In the long run, the market will need to contend with the transaction and environmental costs currently associated with using crypto technology. We will also need to establish more explicit legal frameworks around NFT ownership and clarify how NFTs relate to existing forms of ownership rights—especially around intellectual property. At the same time, it's likely that the most valuable applications of NFTs haven't even been envisioned yet.

Nevertheless, the community-based NFT projects that have taken off so far give a hint of what may be to come.

NFTs enable new markets by allowing people to create and build upon new forms of ownership. These projects succeed by leveraging a core dynamic of crypto: A token's worth comes from users' shared agreement, and this means that the community one builds around NFTs quite literally creates those NFTs' underlying value. And the more these communities increase engagement and become part of people's personal identities, the more that value is reinforced.

Newer applications will take greater advantage of online-offline connections and introduce increasingly complex token designs. But even today, it's less surprising than you might think that people are making money selling pictures on the internet.

Amid a flood of new NFT ventures, it can be hard to tell which have merit and which are just riding the hype. But there is a logic to how—and when—they create value. Companies that have been most successful in this new frontier are able to:

- ✓ **Make meaningful use of the NFT technology itself.** NFTs make less sense when there isn't a purpose to digital ownership (such as managing physical collectibles).
- ✓ **Leverage a community of users.** Lack of engagement can become a self-fulfilling prophecy, devaluing the NFTs themselves.

- ✓ **Generate confidence that they can continue executing.** Teams must communicate frequently and transparently about how they intend to evolve the project.
- ✓ **Offer on-ramps for new users.** "Submerging" crypto technology allows new users to engage with NFTs more easily.
- ✓ **Stay resilient amid crypto market swings.** Price volatility and an evolving regulatory framework are inevitable.

Adapted from content posted on hbr.org, November 10, 2021 (product #H06OR1).

HOW YOUR BRAND SHOULD USE NFTs

by Arun Sundararajan

NFTs could be the killer app of Web3 and its gateway into traditional commerce. The *really* interesting thing about NFTs is the tech they run on, which reveals their broader promise as a vehicle by which brands bypass the platform-centric marketing world of Web2 and reclaim ownership of their digital consumer relationships.

Early Days: From Collectibles to Digital Product-Line Extensions

Right now, NFTs seem inextricably intertwined with digital collectibles, and many brands' first step into the NFT waters has thus been to launch their own collections. These early efforts range from exclusive releases of Campbell's Soup–can art and Coca-Cola digital apparel to generative art of burgers from White Castle.

But a first step isn't a strategy. Successful brands didn't call it a day after buying a domain name and posting a website in the dot-com era, and similarly, smart brands need to be asking themselves what comes next.

The answer will present itself more readily for some brands than others, just as it did when 1990s brick-and-mortar companies sought meaningful ways to use the internet. Back then, retailers with a catalog business, like Office Depot, were able to start using the internet as a channel more quickly than other companies because they already had the infrastructure for taking orders and making deliveries. The e-commerce journey of bookstores like Barnes & Noble was simpler than those of apparel, furniture, or grocery retailers because they sold books—easy to describe, of a convenient form factor, nonperishable, and presenting no issues of user "fit."

There's a similar dynamic at play in the NFT world. Companies in the media business can naturally use NFTs to create a new class of media assets. NBA's Top Shot is the most compelling legacy example of this kind of product-line expansion. Analogously, apparel companies can envisage digital versions of their physical clothing and accessories. Ralph Lauren has already been selling branded digital apparel in virtual worlds like Zepeto. Dolce & Gabbana auctioned millions of dollars' worth of NFT-based digital couture.

Each of these projects ports a current product line into the metaverse, expanding how consumers engage with and experience the brands. The transition is especially seamless for sneaker companies already steeped in the NFT lingo of drops and flipping. Nike has gone as far as acquiring RTFKT, a startup specializing in NFT-based digital sneakers, while Adidas has created a line of virtual gear for the characters of NFT leader Bored Ape Yacht Club.

The Real Promise: NFTs as the Basis for a Multifaceted Digital Consumer Connection

Extending product lines into digital worlds is just one possible use for NFTs, however. Companies that bind

NFT thinking exclusively to collectibles or creating digital assets for virtual avatars are missing a more important shift. Looking ahead a few years, NFTs could be the central digital touchpoint between brands and their consumers—and one that is controlled by the brand itself.

While NFTs are mostly being used for unique *digital* assets, the underlying technology could just as well identify a unique experience (the fact that you attended an event, for example) or a unique *physical-world* object. It's a question of how companies use the digital identifier that forms the basis for each NFT's assertion of uniqueness and authenticity. For instance, Nike's 2019 CryptoKick patent connects a physical pair of shoes to an NFT-based virtual twin, setting up a future in which owners of multiple sneaker NFTs might even "breed" them into custom kicks. Emerging technologies like those from Veracity Protocol facilitate the creation of digital identifiers encodable into an NFT that are derived from the actual material or structural properties of the physical items in question.

Such NFT-encoded digital identifiers can chronicle a whole host of real-world purchase and consumption experiences, infusing them into our digital lives in ways that are authentic and portable across communities, and creating exciting new possibilities for brands and their consumers. Designed right, NFTs could build on the expansion of conspicuous consumption seeded by social media, allowing us to showcase our nondigital lives in our digital spaces more expansively and more authentically. Did you stand in line to buy the new iPhone on the day it was released? Attend a concert by that popular band before they were famous? Or are you simply interested in sharing your extensive brand-name wardrobe with your digital friends in a way that is natural and understated? Future virtual spaces could feature your NFTs of each of these purchases or experiences, providing presentation options tailored to your preferred level of subtlety or ostentation that transcend today's narrow alternatives of Facebook check-ins and Reddit profile badges.

These blockchain-based tokens of authenticity could also revolutionize secondary markets for physical items. Thus far, original manufacturers have rarely captured value when their items are resold, and in these rare cases of value capture (like certified-pre-owned vehicles), the items must be expensive enough to justify the overhead of certification and sales. An NFT-based digital seal of authenticity for a physical item creates more seamless trust in peer-to-peer resale and can empower a brand to share in the associated value capture more easily using platforms like Trove and Recurate that integrate this kind of secondary trading into a branded retail experience. Since NFTs are not just static digital records of authenticity, but are programmable, brands might even implement an NFT royalty standard that encodes a small fraction of value capture associated with every resale.

Brands should also consider how some things of value are unique but not scarce. Minting an NFT with each consumer transaction can create a dynamic digital point of contact specific to that transaction that can respond to a range of external events and signals. The possibilities for new and creative loyalty and after-sale engagement are endless.

Brands' Paths Toward an NFT Future

It's easy to forget how long it took established companies to figure out how to navigate Web1 and make meaningful connections between the internet channel and their existing businesses. Walmart started actively selling online only in 2000, a full six years after Amazon's founding. As late as 2001, other retailing titans like Target, still struggling with e-commerce operations, chose to rely on Amazon's storefront and fulfillment capabilities, laying the foundations for Amazon's immense platform business.

And Web3 is developing more slowly than Web1 and Web2 as a commercial technological infrastructure, in part because of an ethos among some of the community to actively resist the centralized coordination that can accelerate that evolution. As such, the true brand possibilities of NFTs will take a few years to realize.

Nevertheless, much like in the early days of the Web, it is critical for brands to simultaneously ensure that they don't fall behind, while also not succumbing to misguided choices that look like "checking off the NFT box."

Start with Smart Digital Collectibles

It's a safe bet that the immediate NFT mindset will remain centered around digital collectibles. During this phase, it's important to engineer the right tradeoffs between availability and exclusivity when creating an NFT collection. For instance, the rarity of the Campbell's and Coca-Cola NFTs may make sustaining consumer interest a challenge. On the other hand, making your NFT collection too abundant can lead to a perception of insufficient value. The desire for collectibles is mimetic—value stems from enough people wanting what others want. Striking the right balance is critical.

Exclusivity is just one lever that shapes consumer interest. Brands can also leverage the programmability of NFTs to make them more collaborative and engaging. Gap has gamified its NFTs collection by allowing multiple common NFTs to be combined into fewer limited ones. Integrating community features into an NFT collection can further enhance engagement. Social value is partly why the Bored Ape Yacht Club is sustaining greater interest levels (and valuations) than its CryptoPunks predecessor.

Tie Your NFT Collection to Your Brand and Core Product

Most brands don't aspire, long term, to remain in the business of creating and selling digital art. Connecting your NFT collection to your brand identity is essential, like Nivea has done with its non-fungible touch collection. Brand perception can also be enhanced with a novel philanthropic dimension. Budweiser's sponsoring of 22 rising musicians via its Royalty NFTs creatively uses the capabilities of NFT technology for micro-sponsorship, allowing the brand to rise above the more prosaic philanthropy of "donating the proceeds of my NFT drop" that numerous others have already tried.

While lamenting the glacial consumerization of the underlying Web3 technology, you can nevertheless start to strengthen NFT connections with your products or services in small ways. Invert the idea of an NFT as a digital token of physical product ownership by giving away a physical product tied to a digital NFT collectible. When Coach launched an NFT collection featuring art of animals from its holiday promotions, it also promised a custom Coach bag to each NFT holder. Connect NFT issuance to participation in brand-associated experiences (events you sponsor, for example). Mint NFTs that document attendance of exclusive branded experiences like product launch events or fashion shows. Enhance an existing loyalty program with an NFT collection, like Clinique has done.

Experiment, but with Authenticity and an Eye on the Future

Wading into the murky waters of Web3 will seem daunting at first. Over time, brands must figure out what works for them through trial and error and observing what succeeds and fails for others. Remember that much like with Web1 and Web2, earnest adoption and experimentation will attract greater rewards. Feigning community membership by co-opting NFT slang in social media posts can backfire by making you appear out of touch, and token NFT art collection efforts will probably get you as far as your dot-com era vanity websites did.

Making Sense of the NFT Marketplace

by Pavel Kireyev and Peter C. Evans

Both individual creators and firms as wide-ranging as retail, music, entertainment, consumer products, fashion, and more have begun actively exploring ways to engage with the world of NFTs. While some sellers have opted to build their own NFT marketplaces, most have found that a partnership with a third-party platform is more feasible, as it can reduce up-front costs, offer access to a larger existing customer base, and provide valuable add-on services such as marketing, legal, and technical support.

When it comes to leveraging a rapidly evolving new technology like NFTs, it's not always obvious what the right choice is. To avoid making costly mistakes, it's critical to understand the landscape of platforms that are currently available and determine which will be the best fit for your NFT offerings.

We've found that it can be particularly helpful to characterize NFT marketplaces on a spectrum from *streamlined* to *augmented*. Streamlined marketplaces support a broader range of NFTs and offer more limited, generic services to sellers, while augmented marketplaces are highly specialized and provide a more full-service experience.

Streamlined platforms include services such as OpenSea and Rarible, which host both auctions and fixed-price sales for a wide variety of NFTs, and more closely resemble traditional platforms such as eBay, Esty, or Mercari. These marketplaces focus predominantly on enabling efficient transactions, often providing payment infrastructure to accept both credit cards and crypto payments. They offer minimal additional services, and because of their breadth, these platforms generally have fairly large and varied user bases.

Augmented marketplaces, on the other hand, tend to focus on narrower niches and offer numerous value-added services such as minting (creating the NFT itself), marketing, curation, pricing recommendations, portfolio trackers, and even full-blown games built on top of the NFTs. For example, Sorare, which focuses on digital sports cards, hosts fantasy soccer competitions that incorporate the cards users buy on the platform.

(continued)

Making Sense of the NFT Marketplace

These specialty services can add a lot of value, but of course, they come at a cost. To account for the resources required to build out, integrate, and support an array of customized tools and experiences, augmented platforms generally have a higher "take rate," or transaction fee, as well as higher up-front setup costs. Streamlined marketplaces typically have lower initial and ongoing costs but may require sellers to invest their own resources or hire external experts to design, mint, and market their NFTs.

So, if you're a creator, don't feel like you have to wait for the "Amazon of NFTs" to emerge. Evaluate the marketplaces that are currently available based on how well they fit with your unique offerings and business needs, and if you find one that seems well suited for you, go ahead and dip in a toe.

Adapted from content posted on hbr.org, November 18, 2021 (product #H06PH9).

The good news is that the true impact of NFTs will unfold gradually over the next few years, and there's plenty of time to figure out the space. Your eventual audience is the entirety of your existing and future customers, not today's crypto community. So don't measure success by your NFT prices on OpenSea. Rather, orient your metrics toward those that better illuminate a future in which NFTs anchor all real-world products and experiences while extending them into the digital world of your choosing.

Wading into the NFT space can be daunting for brands, but as companies learned in the early days of the internet, there's also risk in not engaging at all. Now is the time to plan and experiment.

- ✓ Releasing collectible NFTs is a good place to start, but it's also just a first step.
- ✓ Exclusivity is just one lever that shapes consumer interest. Brands can also leverage the programmability of NFTs to make them more collaborative and engaging.
- ✓ Look for ways to tie your NFT project to your brand and core product. Brand perception can also be enhanced with a novel philanthropic dimension. Invert the idea of an NFT as a digital

token of physical product ownership by giving away a physical product tied to a digital NFT collectible.

✓ Experiment, but with authenticity and an eye on the future. There's little to gain here by trying to mimic what others are doing if it feels obviously out of step with your brand.

Adapted from content posted on hbr.org, February 28, 2022 (product #H06VU0).

Section 3

THE ROAD TO WEB3

8

PLATFORMS NEED TO WORK WITH THEIR USERS—NOT AGAINST THEM

by Ethan Bueno de Mesquita and Andrew Hall

As we write, thousands of online communities created for a wide variety of purposes—everything from providing crypto financial services to crowdsourcing art collecting—are building new democracies and rapidly evolving systems for discussion, debate, voting, and representation. This movement, often known as Web3, has created an explosion of interest in giving ownership and decision-making power to community participants rather than to a small number of business executives.

This phenomenon highlights a critical challenge for traditional platforms like Amazon, Meta, Google's play store, and Apple's app store, gaming platforms like Roblox or Steam, and even for newer centralized crypto platforms like Coinbase and OpenSea. Historically, as platforms became dominant in their domain, they raised fees and changed rules to their benefit and their producers' loss. They could do so because those producers—software developers, small retailers, game designers, or content creators—had nowhere else to go. But once learned, twice a fool: How can platforms keep producers making new investments in building for environments whose undemocratic governance systems cannot credibly promise to reflect their interests in the long run?

There is a way. By granting *governance tokens* to producers that give them the unbreakable right to vote on key decisions about fees and rules, platforms can give producers the ownership and assurances they need to unleash their innovation—to the benefit of the platform, its users, and its creative partners.

We are academics who study democratic systems of governance, and we are also advisers in the tech sector who think about the future of decentralized governance. In this essay, we'll explain the challenge platforms are facing in maximizing the efforts of their producers, we'll show how insights from blockchain governance can help, and we'll discuss some specifics of how to implement a governance-token system that avoids common pitfalls that democracies have been grappling with for thousands of years.

The Lock-in Problem

In the early days of Web 2.0—the movement that gave us mega platforms like Amazon, Facebook, and Uber—producers flocked to build new platforms because that's where the users, and thus the profits, were. But as some platforms failed and others became dominant in their spaces, the producers' outside options dwindled, and so did their market power.

Today, it's all but impossible for an app developer to succeed without selling to iPhone users. A handicraft company that doesn't list on Etsy loses access to a huge pool of potential buyers. A person who specializes in creating content that builds a large following on Instagram cannot easily replicate their success on another social media platform. And so on.

In all of these cases, the creators' bargaining position vis-à-vis the platform is substantially weaker than it used to be. And the platforms leveraged this weakness, raising fees and changing rules in ways that benefit the platforms at the expense of the producers who helped them become dominant. This is what economists call "the holdup problem": When creators become locked into dominant platforms, those dominant platforms can hold them up.

In the short run, the holdup problem harms producers. But in the long run, it actually hurts platform owners, too. Because producers anticipate that platform owners will exploit increasing market power, they are less willing to invest in making the products that bring users to the platform in the first place. And that makes the platforms themselves less valuable.

How Decentralized Governance Can Help

Decentralized governance models pioneered in the crypto space can reassure producers that they can invest their efforts without fearing future expropriation. These models hold great promise, and they underpin the way that Bitcoin and Ethereum run their blockchains, as well as the way that decentralized autonomous organizations (or DAOs) with billions of dollars' worth of commitments, like MakerDAO or Uniswap, operate their protocols.

Applying decentralized governance to major platforms is straightforward conceptually. If a major platform owner made a credible commitment that its fee structure could not be changed without a vote of the platform's producers, then those producers would be reassured that their profits would not be eroded in the future, even as the platform became more successful and increased in market power. Thus the producers would be more willing to invest, attracting users and benefiting both themselves and the platform owner.

How would this work in practice?

Taking inspiration from blockchain governance, platforms can create a system of democratic governance built around a governance token that assigns voting rights to producers. In this model, each token that a person holds guarantees them one vote on key decisions governed by this decentralized system. To make these votes especially secure and credibly protected from interference by the platform, the token itself could live on a major layer-1 blockchain, like Ethereum, which would make it impossible for the platform to unduly alter token ownership or interfere with the outcomes of on-chain votes.

A few details are important. First, tokens are granted for value creation, so the more value a producer has brought to the platform, the more power they have over governance decisions. Second, tokens are transferable—that is, a token holder can give some agent their proxy or can sell their vote (perhaps within certain limits). Third, there are many possible voting systems (among them, majority rule, supermajority rule, and approval voting) with various costs and benefits. The voting system itself would have to be specified up front, though it might also allow for a procedure for considering changes to the voting rule itself. Finally, the platform owner would continue to hold proposal power: Although the token holders would have the right to accept or reject proposals, the proposals themselves would come from the platform owners. Platform owners would thus know that changes couldn't be forced on them.

Risks and Challenges

Such a system offers substantial benefits but also raises questions. We focus on four that have cropped up in both blockchain governance and democracy in the physical world.

Will giving producers voting power solve the holdup problem better than other approaches?

Perhaps the most obvious approach to solving the holdup problem is a traditional contract between platform owners and producers that locks in fee structures or veto rights. But such a contract only solves the holdup problem to the extent that producers believe they can afford to enforce that contract against larger and more deep-pocketed platforms.

By contrast, a smart contract implemented on the blockchain can make it impossible for platform owners to implement a change of rules for on-platform business unless a sufficient number of token holders have approved that change. Thus tokenized governance creates the commitment needed to solve the holdup problem, even if the two sides aren't equally matched in court.

Even with tokenized governance, a platform could choose to shut down the entire voting system in the future. While this risk can never be fully mitigated, such a public and large-scale contractual breach might be more easily litigated than the specifics of fees and rules. And the public nature of the voting system would also make doing so reputationally costly, especially for public-facing platforms.

What if producers vote in their own narrow self-interest and harm the platform as a result?

Giving producers veto power over changes to the rules of commerce on the platform creates the risk that the platform might not be able to make critical changes to its business model. Making a credible commitment to producers necessarily entails at least some business risk.

But tokenized governance offers safeguards against the most worrying downsides for two reasons. First, as we've pointed out, producers who have the most at stake in the success of the platform will have the most voting power. Second, governance tokens can be traded. This means that if the platform needs to make a change that producers oppose, it can buy the necessary votes from those producers. In this way, the governance system provides exactly the right kind of safeguard—it allows platforms to make critical changes that might harm producers, but only if those changes are so important that the platform is willing to compensate the producers for their losses by buying their votes.

Of course, not every producer who opposes the new rule will be compensated, since the platform only needs to buy the bare minimum of votes necessary to get approval. Under simple majority rule, the platform only has to buy half the total votes. Under more stringent supermajority rules, the platform must buy a larger percentage of votes. Thus one important consideration in the choice of a voting rule is how to balance the tradeoff between a system that provides broad compensation for producers who are harmed by rule changes and a system that provides enough flexibility that platform owners will not be stymied in making necessary changes to the business model.

What if participation in governance is too low?

Giving governance power to producers won't work if they don't use it. Getting people to participate in democracy is an age-old problem, and it has predictably cropped up in blockchain governance.

A well-designed token for platform governance can address this problem in several ways. For example, large token holders—who possess the most voting power—will care a lot about the policy decisions they are voting on and so will have strong incentives to participate. The token itself can also provide direct incentives for participation, by providing token holders with dividends in exchange for participating or by revoking ("burning") their tokens if they fail to participate too many times. There are still other ways to encourage participation—by building easy electronic-voting systems that reduce the cognitive and time costs of voting, by performing outreach around important votes, and by creating norms that encourage token holders to participate.

In addition to working to encourage participation, the system could also have built-in safeguards such as quorum rules that mean votes of the token holders are only binding on the platform when a sufficient level of participation is reached.

What if the voting process is corrupted through bribery or other means?

Instituting votes over decisions with real economic stakes immediately raises concern about governance attacks. Blockchain governance has seen many issues like this. Malicious actors have bought up voting power and used it to line their own pockets, and even hacked insecure smart contracts to take over protocols.

A governance attack by a competing platform that bought up voting rights to block important policy changes would be particularly worrying. Thoughtful design is required to mitigate these risks.

One strategy would be to restrict the transferability of tokens so that votes could only be cast by verified producers or the platform itself. Of course, this wouldn't prevent more standard vote buying by malicious actors. But it would substantially raise the costs of a governance attack by requiring malicious actors to make separate arrangements with many decentralized voters and solve their own commitment problem vis-à-vis those voters.

A second strategy, which does not require restricted transferability, involves imposing a lockup period prior to voting during which governance tokens could not be transferred. Such a lockup period would ensure that platforms are not taken by surprise by a governance attack.

Conclusion

The blockchain/crypto space is frothy at the moment, and there is no doubt that many experiments in democratizing online platforms will prove to be dead ends. But Web3 has momentum: People want more control over the online communities that they belong to and that they often depend on for their economic livelihoods. In the coming years, it will be crucial to understand where and how it makes sense to democratize the governance of a wide variety of business enterprises. Major platforms have an opportunity to lead the way, while benefiting both themselves and those who operate in the ecosystems they create.

Once the giant tech platforms of the Web 2.0 era became dominant, they raised fees and changed rules to their benefit and their producers' loss. In the long run, it also hurt the platforms themselves, because producers won't continue to invest in platforms that work against their interests. Web3 promises a path to avoiding this trap.

- ✓ Granting governance tokens to producers would give them the unbreakable right to vote on key decisions, giving them the ownership and assurances they need to unleash their innovation.
- ✓ These tokens would be granted for value creation, so the more value a producer has brought to the platform, the more power they would have over governance decisions.

- ✓ Platforms will need to manage risks and challenges to a democratic system including low participation, producers voting with narrow self-interests, and the possibility of corruption or bribery.

Adapted from content posted on hbr.org, May 5, 2022 (product #H070TS).

9

CAUTIONARY TALES FROM CRYPTOLAND

An interview with Molly White by Tom Stackpole

Suddenly it feels like Web3 is everywhere. The money, the buzz, the *name* all make it seem like Web3 will inevitably be the next big thing. But is it? And do we even want it to be?

As the hype has reached a fever pitch, critics have started to warn of unintended and overlooked consequences of a web with a blockchain backbone. And while Web3 advocates focus on what the future of the internet *could* be, skeptics such as Molly White, a software developer and Wikipedia editor, are focused on the very real problems of the here and now.

White created the website Web3 Is Going Just Great, a timeline that tracks scams, hacks, rug pulls, collapses, shady dealings, and other examples of problems with Web3. HBR.org's tech editor Tom Stackpole spoke to White over email about what people aren't hearing about Web3, how blockchain could make internet harassment much worse, and why the whole project might be, as the site's tagline puts it, "an enormous grift that's pouring lighter fluid on our already smoldering planet." This interview has been lightly edited.

HBR: ***You make it very clear that you don't have a financial stake in Web3 one way or another. So what led you to start your project and write about Web3's problems?***

MOLLY WHITE: Late 2021 was when I really began to notice a huge shift in how people talk about crypto. Instead of being primarily used for speculative investments by people who were willing to take on a lot of risk in exchange for hopes of huge returns, people began to talk about how the whole web was going to shift toward services that were built using blockchains. Everyone would have a crypto wallet, and everyone would adopt these new blockchain-based projects for social networks, video games, online communities, and so on.

This shift got my attention, because until then crypto had always felt fairly "opt-in" to me. It was previously a somewhat niche technology, even to software engineers, and it seemed like the majority of people who engaged with it financially were fairly aware of the volatility risks. Those of us who didn't want anything to do with crypto could just not put any money into it.

Once crypto began to be marketed as something that everyone would need to engage with, and once projects began trying to bring in broader, more mainstream audiences—often people who didn't seem to understand the technology or the financial risks—I got very concerned. Blockchains are not well suited to many, if not most, of the use cases that are being described as "Web3," and I have a lot of concerns about the implications of them being used in that way. I also saw just an enormous number of crypto and Web3 projects going terribly: people coming up with incredibly poorly thought-out project ideas and people and companies alike losing tons of money to scams, hacks, and user error.

In the examples you've collected, what are some of the common mistakes or misapprehensions you see in companies' efforts to launch Web3 projects, whether they're NFTs or something else?

My overwhelming feeling is that Web3 projects seem to be a solution in search of a problem. It often seems like project creators knew they wanted to incorporate blockchains somehow and then went casting around for some problem they could try to solve with a blockchain without much thought as to whether it was the right technology to address it, or even if the problem was something that could or should be solved with technology at all.

Kickstarter might have been the most egregious example of this: Late in 2021 it announced, much to the chagrin of many in its user base, that it would be completely rebuilding its platform on a blockchain. A few months later, an interview to explain the decision, COO Sean Leow gave the distinct impression that he had no idea why Kickstarter was reimplementing its platform this way—what governance problems it was trying to solve, why a blockchain would be effective in solving them.[1]

Companies also seem to announce NFT projects without doing much research into how these have gone for other companies in their sector. We've seen enough NFT announcements by video game studios that have gone so badly that they've chosen to reverse the decision within days or even hours. And yet somehow a new game company will do this and then be surprised at the backlash over NFTs' considerable carbon footprint or the sense that they're just a grift. The same is true for ostensibly environmentally conscious organizations announcing NFTs—even in some cases projects that are entirely focused on environmentalism, like the World Wildlife Fund, which tried and failed to launch a less carbon-intensive NFT series.

I firmly believe that companies first need to identify and research the problem they are trying to solve, and *then* select the right technology to do it. Those technologies may not be the latest buzzword, and they may not cause venture capitalists to come crawling out of the woodwork, but choosing technologies with that approach tends to be a lot more successful in the long run—at least, assuming the primary goal is to actually solve a problem rather than attract VC money.

One of the most surprising (to me, anyway) arguments you make is that Web3 could be a disaster for privacy and create major issues around harassment. Why? And does it feel like the companies "buying into" Web3 are aware of this?

Blockchains are immutable, which means once data is recorded, it can't be removed. The idea that blockchains will be used to store user-generated data for services like social networks has enormous implications for user safety. If someone uses these platforms to harass and abuse others, such as by doxing, posting revenge pornography, uploading child sexual abuse material, or doing any number of other very serious things that platforms normally try to thwart with content-moderation teams, the protections that can be offered to users are extremely limited. The same goes for users who plagiarize artwork, spam, or share sensitive material like trade secrets. Even a user who themself posts something and then later decides they'd rather not have it online is stuck with it remaining on-chain indefinitely.

Many blockchains also have a very public record of transactions: Anyone can see that a person made a transaction and the details of that transaction. Privacy is theoretically provided through pseudonymity—wallets are identified by a string of characters that aren't inherently tied to a person. But because you'll likely use one wallet for most of your transactions, keeping one's wallet address private can be both challenging and a lot of work and is likely to only become more challenging if this future vision of crypto ubiquity is realized. If a person's wallet address is known and they are using a popular chain like Ethereum to transact, anyone [else] can see all transactions they've made.

Imagine if you went on a first date, and when you paid them back for your half of the meal, they could now see every other transaction you'd ever made—not just the public transactions on some app you used to transfer the cash but *any* transactions: the split checks with all of your previous dates, that monthly transfer to your therapist, the debts you're paying off (or not), the charities to which you're donating (or not), the amount you're putting in a retirement account (or not). What if they could see the location of the corner store by your apartment where you so frequently go to grab a pint of ice cream at 10 p.m.? And this would also be visible to your ex-partners, your estranged family members, your prospective employers, or any number of outside parties interested in collecting your data and using it for any purpose they like. If you had a stalker or had left an abusive relationship or were the target of harassment, the granular details of your life are right there.

There are some blockchains that try to obfuscate these types of details for privacy purposes. But there are tradeoffs here: While transparency can enable harassment, the features that make it possible to achieve privacy in a trustless system also enable financial crimes like money laundering. It is also very difficult to use those currencies (and to cash them out to traditional forms of currency). There are various techniques that people can use to try to remain anonymous, but they tend to require technical skill and quite a lot of work on the user's end to maintain that anonymity.

This point of view seems almost totally absent from the conversation. Why do you think that is?

I think a lot of companies haven't put much thought into the technology's abuse potential. I'm surprised at how often I bring it up and the person I'm talking to admits that it's never crossed their mind.

When the abuse potential is acknowledged, there's a very common sentiment in the Web3 space that these fundamental problems are just minor issues that can be fixed later, without any acknowledgment that they are intrinsic characteristics of the technology that can't easily be changed after the fact. I believe it's completely unacceptable to release products without any apparent thought to this vector of user risk, and so I am shocked when companies take that view.

One of the mainstays of the pitch made by Web3 proponents is that blockchain can democratize (or re-democratize) the web and provide new sources of wealth and opportunity—even banking the unbanked. What's your take on that?

It's a compelling pitch; I'll give them that. But crypto has so far been enormously successful at taking wealth from the average person or the financially disadvantaged and "redistributing" it to the already wealthy. The arguments I've seen for how this same technology is suddenly going to result in the democratization of wealth have been enormously uncompelling. The emerging crypto space is very poorly regulated, especially the newer parts of it pertaining to decentralized finance. It's difficult for me to see a future where poorly regulated technology with built-in perverse financial incentives will magically result in fairer, more accessible systems.

As for "banking the unbanked" and the democratization of the web, people are falling into a trap that technologists have fallen into over and over again: trying to solve social problems purely with technology. People are not unbanked because of some technological failure. People lack access to banking services for all sorts of reasons: They don't have money to open a bank account to begin with, they're undocumented, they don't have access to a physical bank or an internet or mobile connection, or they don't trust banks due to high levels of corruption in their financial or judicial systems.

These are not problems that can be solved solely through the addition of a blockchain. Indeed, crypto solutions introduce even *more* barriers: the technological know-how and the level of security practices required to safeguard a crypto wallet; the knowledge and time to try to distinguish "scammy" projects from those that are trying to be legitimate; the lack of consumer protections if something happens to an exchange where you are keeping your funds; and the added difficulty of reversing fraud when it does occur.

In my view, the places where crypto has done some good—and I do openly acknowledge that it has done some good—have primarily been in situations where there are enormous societal and political failings, and *any* replacement is better than what exists. For example, some people have successfully used crypto to send remittances to people under oppressive regimes. These examples are fairly limited, and the fact that it's worked seems largely because crypto hasn't been deployed in such a widespread way for those regimes to try to become involved.

Given all of this, what do you think is the cultural draw of Web3?

The ideological argument for Web3 is very compelling, and I personally hold many of the same ideals. I *strongly* believe in working toward a more equitable and accessible financial system, creating a fairer distribution of wealth in society, supporting artists and creators, ensuring privacy and control over one's data, and democratizing access to the web. These are all things you will hear Web3 projects claiming to try to solve.

I just don't think that creating technologies based around cryptocurrencies and blockchains is the solution to these problems. These technologies build up financial barriers; they don't knock them down. They seek to introduce a layer of financialization to everything we do that I feel is, in many ways, worse than the existing systems they seek to replace. These are social and societal issues, not technological ones, and the solutions will be found in societal and political change.

Should HBR Press even be doing this book? Are we buying into—or amplifying—the hype cycle?

I think we are comfortably beyond the "ignore it and hope it goes away" phase of crypto. I know I decided I was beyond that phase late in 2021. I think the best thing that journalists who report on crypto can do at this stage is ask the tough questions, seek out experts wherever they can, and try not to fall for the boosterism.

Crypto and Web3 are complex on so many levels—technologically, economically, sociologically, legally—that it is difficult for any single person to report on all issues, but there are extremely competent people who have examined crypto through each of these lenses and who are asking those tough questions.

One of the biggest failures of the media in reporting on crypto has been uncritically reprinting statements from crypto boosters with little reflection on the legitimacy or feasibility of those statements. It doesn't have to be that way. That is not to say that there needs to be a double standard, either—I think most, if not all, crypto skeptics welcome pushback and critical editing of what they say and write (though I do think the financial incentive to be skeptical of crypto is dwarfed compared to the incentive to be positive about it).

Kevin Roose suggested in "The Latecomer's Guide to Crypto" in the Sunday *New York Times* in early 2022 that, in the Web 2.0 era, the early skeptics were to blame for the ills of social media because they weren't "loud enough" in their skepticism.[2] I would counter that they were not given the opportunity to be as loud as they wanted to be and that those who did hear them did not listen, or at least did not meaningfully act upon what they heard. Perhaps there is an opportunity for history not to repeat itself.

Web3 optimists bluster about progress on the horizon, but at present the space is rife with fraud, hacks, and collapses. Web3 critic Molly White, interviewed here by HBR, believes that as the technology becomes more mainstream, its ability to do harm—financial, emotional, and reputational—will grow, and fast.

- ✓ Blockchain technology is often applied in ways, or to problems, to which it is not well-suited, and companies frequently don't understand the consequences of their decision to utilize it.
- ✓ Privacy concerns around immutable records on blockchains, which could make it more difficult to address online harassment, are widely being overlooked.
- ✓ Despite the arguments proponents make about opportunity and democratization, crypto projects so far have mostly served the rich and powerful.
- ✓ Now is the moment for Web3 skeptics to raise their voices—early skeptics of the harms caused by

> social media in the emergence of Web 2.0 were not heard, and there is an opportunity not to make the same mistakes this time.

Adapted from content posted on hbr.org, May 10, 2022 (product #H071AM).

NOTES

1. Beat staff, "Kickstarter Exec on Blockchain Backlash: 'We've Learned a Hell of a Lot in the Last Couple of Months,'" Beat, February 18, 2022, https://www.comicsbeat.com/kickstarter-blockchain-controversy-interview/.

2. Kevin Roose, "The Latecomer's Guide to Crypto," *New York Times*, March 18, 2022, https://www.nytimes.com/interactive/2022/03/18/technology/cryptocurrency-crypto-guide.html.

10

HOW DAOs COULD CHANGE THE WAY WE WORK

by Steve Glaveski

Every technological revolution has transformed the way we work. The plow turned hunter-gatherers into farmers. The spinning jenny and the power loom turned farmers into factory workers. Industrial automation and computers turned factory workers into office dwellers, and then the internet fundamentally changed the way we got work done. And now, there's a new transformation on the horizon that promises to change the way we work again: Web3.

Web3 represents the next iteration of the World Wide Web. It's built upon blockchain technology and cryptocurrencies, and is characterized by greater decentralization, transparency, and shared ownership. As venture capital firm Andreesen Horowitz's general partner Chris Dixon tweeted, Web1 was read-only (directories), Web2 was read-write (social media), and Web3 is read-write-*own*.[1] The decentralized autonomous organization, or DAO, is set to be the vehicle that leads the charge.

DAOs are effectively owned and governed by people who hold a sufficient number of a DAO's native token, which functions like a type of cryptocurrency. For example, $FWB is the native token of the popular social DAO called Friends With Benefits, and people can buy, earn, or trade it. There are many different permutations of DAOs, with some being more decentralized than others. DAOs run the gamut from media organizations, to venture funds and grant programs, to social networks, video games, financial and tech platforms, and philanthropic efforts.

So how exactly could DAOs change the way we work?

More Autonomy Over Where, When, and How We Work

As DAOs proliferate, instead of having one employer and a 40-hour workweek, we might contribute several hours a week to several DAOs. This is already typical among early adopters to the space. Today's creator economy, populated by vloggers, bloggers, and podcasters, can give us a glimpse into what the Web3 working world might look like, with the typical creator earning income from a variety of projects such as coaching, consulting, and content monetization on various platforms such as YouTube, SubStack, and Patreon.

Freedom to Do More Fulfilling Work

The technology-centric nature of DAOs may result in rudimentary, algorithmic work being automated, freeing up contributors to be the most creative and useful versions of themselves and allowing them to spend more time on high-value activities—the type that stimulate the flow state—and less time on monotonous, shallow tasks.

While 85% of today's global workforce is disengaged at work, DAOs will give people more freedom to choose projects whose mission and vision truly resonate with them, jobs that align with their strengths, and values-aligned people to work with.[2] This could also help to mitigate the work-life conflicts, excessive workloads, lack of autonomy, and office politics that drive workplace stress.

More Decision-Making Power

Contributors will be able to use their DAO's native tokens to vote on key decisions. You can get a glimpse into the kinds of decisions DAO members are already voting on at Snapshot, which is essentially a decentralized voting system. Having said this, existing voting mechanisms have been criticized by the likes of Vitalik Buterin, founder of Ethereum.[3] So, this type of voting is likely to evolve over time.

Different Compensation Structures

While DAOs are likely to have a set of core contributors (at least in the early stages) who might be engaged on a full-time basis and even earn salaries, most people contributing to DAOs will instead complete individual tasks, or "bounties," such as "build a messaging app" or "moderate an online community forum." Contributors can work-to-earn (W2E) and generate either native tokens or fiat currency denominated in USDC, a digital currency pegged to the US dollar, or both.

For example, I recently contributed an article to the investment DAO Global Coin Research and earned 30 of its native $GCR tokens. These tokens can be traded on exchanges such as Uniswap for other tokens or fiat currencies, and they represent ownership in a DAO—which is limited by the number of tokens in its token pool, not dissimilar to the total number of shares a corporation is limited by.

Token holders could then use platforms such as Yearn to "stake" their tokens. Staking effectively amounts to depositing tokens into a central liquidity pool where they're used to validate blockchain transactions. Stakers earn APY (annual percentage yield), which effectively amounts to interest.

In the developing world, the play-to-earn (P2E) model, a variation of W2E, is already bearing fruit for an army of teenagers. For example, *Axie Infinity* is a token-based video game where gamers collect, breed, raise, battle, and trade creatures known as Axies. But unlike traditional video games, where players don't actually *own* their characters or peripheral assets such as swords, players *own* their Axies as NFTs and can sell them on the game's marketplace. The average Axie gamer—typically a teenager from the Philippines—earns about $10 to $20 per day playing the game, on par with the country's average salary, while the price of Axies can appreciate over time with some fetching a price of 300 ETH or about $1 million at time of writing. Axie Infinity generated U.S. $1.3 billion revenues in 2021, attributable to Axie marketplace transaction fees and Axie breeding fees.

Another permutation of this model is learn-to-earn (L2E). An example is the platform RabbitHole, which pays you to learn about Web3 applications. And other permutations include create-to-earn (C2E), such as writing articles or designing artwork in exchange for tokens, and use-to-earn (U2E), such as posting comments and engaging with Web3 social media applications such as Minds.

In addition to all of this, token holders can also speculate on their tokens, the price of which might increase in value over time based on supply and demand, much like traditional shares in a company.

Work from Anywhere

DAOs not only don't care where you work, they also don't care when you work or what you look like while you're working—in fact, many contributors are recognized only by their NFT profile pics. Netflix cofounder Marc Randolph said on the *Future Squared* podcast that "in a place where you're evaluated solely on the quality of your work, no one really cares about your appearance."[4]

Instead of working from a central office all year long and having two to four weeks off, most DAO contributors will likely work remotely, bond in virtual social spaces such as CryptoVoxels or The Sandbox, and for several days or weeks a year, get together in real life for inspiring conferences and retreats.

Traditional organizations that demand that their employees go into the office for two to three days a week effectively anchor their employees to life in one place—usually close to a central business district. Firms with such archaic and mobility-limiting positions will likely find it increasingly difficult to win the battle for millennials and, in particular, Gen-Z talent.

Some might argue that DAOs, like many gig economy companies, threaten labor rights, but DAOs themselves are looking to address this. For example, Opolis, a digital employment cooperative, helps DAO contributors and contractors get their health insurance and 401(k) retirement plans in order.

The DAO movement is still in its infancy and has a number of its own challenges to work out when it comes to governance and trust. The mainstream adoption of

Web3 rests upon the resolution of questions related to user experience, security, scalability, and regulatory clarity. However, at the current pace of talent acquisition, capital-raising, and innovation in the space, mainstream proliferation could happen sooner rather than later.

At its core, Web3 promises more fulfilling and outcome-focused work, with a fairer distribution of ownership and rewards—and that is a future worth building.

Web3 promises work that is more fulfilling and focused on outcomes, with a fair distribution of ownership and rewards. The decentralized autonomous organization, or DAO, is set to be the vehicle that leads the charge.

- ✓ DAOs run the gamut from media organizations, to venture funds and grant programs, to social networks, video games, financial and tech platforms, and philanthropic efforts.
- ✓ DAOs are effectively owned and governed by people who hold a sufficient number of a DAO's

native token, which functions like a type of cryptocurrency.

✓ The technology-centric nature of DAOs will result in rudimentary, algorithmic work being automated, freeing up contributors to work from anywhere and be the most creative and useful versions of themselves.

Adapted from content posted on hbr.org, April 7, 2022 (product #H06YZL).

NOTES

1. cdixon.eth, "web1: read, web2: read / write, web3: read / write / own," Twitter, November 11, 2021, https://twitter.com/cdixon/status/1459036992050716697.

2. Jim Harter, "Dismal Employee Engagement Is a Sign of Global Mismanagement," Gallup blog, n.d., https://www.gallup.com/workplace/231668/dismal-employee-engagement-sign-global-mismanagement.aspx.

3. "Moving Beyond Coin Voting Governance," Vitalink, August 16, 2021, https://vitalik.ca/general/2021/08/16/voting3.html.

4. Steve Glaveski, "Episode #366: The Early Days of Netflix with Marc Randolph," October 2019, https://www.nofilter.media/posts/netflix-co-founder-author-and-startup-investor-and-advisor.

About the Contributors

SHAI BERNSTEIN is the Marvin Bower Associate Professor in the Entrepreneurial Management Unit at Harvard Business School and a Faculty Research Fellow at the National Bureau of Economic Research in both the Corporate Finance group and the Productivity, Innovation, and Entrepreneurship group.

ETHAN BUENO DE MESQUITA is the Sydney Stein Professor and deputy dean at the Harris School of Public Policy at the University of Chicago. He is the author or coauthor of three books—*Thinking Clearly with Data*, *Theory and Credibility*, and *Political Economy for Public Policy*—and numerous articles in both political science and economics. He advises tech leaders on issues at the intersection of technology, governance, and society. Follow him on Twitter @ethanbdm.

NIC CARTER is a general partner at Castle Island Ventures, a Cambridge, Massachusetts–based venture firm investing in public blockchain startups, and the cofounder of

Coin Metrics, a blockchain analytics firm. Previously, he served as Fidelity Investments' first cryptoasset analyst.

CHRISTIAN CATALINI is the chief economist of the Diem Association and Diem Networks US, and co-creator of Diem (formerly Libra). He is also the founder of the MIT Cryptoeconomics Lab and a research scientist at MIT.

PETER C. EVANS is the managing partner at the Platform Strategy Institute, chief platform officer of RCRDSHP, and cochair of the MIT Platform Strategy Summit.

STEVE GLAVESKI is the author of *Time Rich: Do Your Best Work, Live Your Best Life* and founder of innovation accelerator Collective Campus and Web3 agency Metavise. He hosts the *Future Squared* and *Metavise* podcasts. Follow him on Twitter @steveglaveski.

ANDREW HALL is a professor of political science at Stanford University and, by courtesy, a professor of political economy at the Stanford Graduate School of Business. He is the codirector of the Democracy and Polarization Lab and a senior fellow at the Stanford Institute for Economic Policy Research. He serves as an adviser to tech companies, investors, and blockchain protocols on issues at the intersection of technology, governance, and society.

MARCO IANSITI is the David Sarnoff Professor of Business Administration at Harvard Business School, where he heads the Technology and Operations Management Unit and the Digital Initiative. He has advised many companies in the technology sector, including Microsoft, Facebook, and Amazon. He is a coauthor (with Karim R. Lakhani) of the book *Competing in the Age of AI* (Harvard Business Review Press, 2020).

STEVE KACZYNSKI is an avid NFT collector who provides NFT market commentary for the Decentralized Generation Network (dgen.network). His professional background is in communications, with a focus on public relations and marketing at large corporations.

PAVEL KIREYEV is an assistant professor of marketing at INSEAD.

SCOTT DUKE KOMINERS is the MBA Class of 1960 Associate Professor of Business Administration in the Entrepreneurial Management Unit at Harvard Business School and a faculty affiliate of the Harvard Department of Economics. He is also an a16z Crypto Research Partner and advises a number of companies on marketplace and incentive design. Previously, he was a junior fellow at the Harvard Society of Fellows and the inaugural Saieh Family Fellow in Economics at the Becker Friedman Institute. Follow him on Twitter @skominers.

KARIM R. LAKHANI is the Charles Edward Wilson Professor of Business Administration and the Dorothy and Michael Hintze Fellow at Harvard Business School and the founder and codirector of the Laboratory for Innovation Science at Harvard. He is a coauthor (with Marco Iansiti) of the book *Competing in the Age of AI* (Harvard Business Review Press, 2020).

OMID MALEKAN is a nine-year veteran of the crypto industry and an adjunct professor at Columbia Business School, where he lectures on blockchain and crypto. He is the author of *Re-Architecting Trust: The Curse of History and the Crypto Cure for Money, Markets, and Platforms.*

JEFF JOHN ROBERTS is crypto editor at *Fortune* and the author of *Kings of Crypto* (Harvard Business Review Press, 2020). His work has appeared in a variety of other publications, including *Bloomberg BusinessWeek*, Reuters, and the *New York Times.* He is an authority on copyright law and other intellectual property issues and is licensed to practice law in New York and Ontario. He has appeared on the BBC, CNN, NBC, CheddarTV, and other media outlets to share his perspectives on technology and the law. Follow him on Twitter @jeffjohnroberts.

JAKE RYAN is the chief investing officer at Tradecraft Capital. He is also the author of *Crypto Asset Investing in the Age of Autonomy.*

THOMAS STACKPOLE is a senior editor at *Harvard Business Review.*

ARUN SUNDARARAJAN is a professor at NYU Stern School of Business who studies how digital technologies transform business and society. Follow him on Twitter @digitalarun.

CHARLES C. Y. WANG is the Glenn and Mary Jane Creamer Associate Professor of Business Administration at Harvard Business School.

MOLLY WHITE is a software developer, Wikipedia editor, and the creator of the website Web3 Is Going Just Great.

Index